T H E

BEATITUDES

The Spiritual Overhauling Kit

BY

DR. OKEY ONUZO

The Beatitudes, The Spiritual Overhauling Kit

ISBN: 978-1-880608-11-1

FIRST EDITION

Published by,

Life Link Worldwide Publishers,

175 Raymond Court Fayetteville GA.

For more information and book orders:

Call:

Email address:

TABLE OF CONTENTS

ACKNOWLEDGMENTS

The messages on the Beatitudes were first shared on the platform of the Kingdom Life Seminar Bible Study series on YouTube, called 'The Antioch Bible Study'. I acknowledge all the brethren who wrote to encourage me each time they received the messages.

Of particular note is Professor Eze Magulike, of the University of Nigeria Teaching Hospital in Enugu, who received the teachings on The Beatitudes through social media and repeatedly encouraged me to turn them into a book.

I acknowledge Nneka Okonkwo for taking the time to transcribe and edit the messages for my review.

I thank my wife Mariam for bearing with me as I laboured on the manuscript day and night.

Above all, I thank the Almighty God for the grace to continue studying the Word of God and the insights He gives along the way.

Okey Onuzo

September 2020

INTRODUCTION

Conforming to the image of Christ is the highest attainment of our Christian calling. It is the heart of the Father's vision that we all become changed into the image of His Son, our Lord, and Saviour Jesus Christ. In Romans 8:29, we read: *"For whom He did foreknow, He also predestined to be conformed into the image of His son, that our Lord Jesus Christ will be the firstborn of many brethren."*

The Bible reveals that our Lord Jesus Christ chose His disciples first to be with Him as told in Mark 3:13-15 (NKJV)

And He went up on the mountain and called to Him those He Himself wanted. And they came to Him. Then He appointed twelve, that they might be with

Him and that He might send them out to preach, and to have power to heal sicknesses and to cast out demons:

The Sermon on the Mount, best collated in Matthew chapters 5 to 7, shows the various dimensions of the new life we received in Christ to which each disciple is called. The first part of the teaching is the Beatitudes. The Beatitudes are the overhauling kit to change the raw believer's character and transform him from a citizen of the world to a heaven-bound citizen. Seven out of the eight declare the blessedness and joy of the person who stops to acquire these new attitudes to life.

O how happy are the poor in spirit: how happy are those who mourn for their sins in deep repentance: how happy are the meek: how happy are those who hunger and thirst after righteousness: how happy are the merciful: how happy are the pure in heart and how happy are the peacemakers. The eighth speak to those being persecuted for righteousness, encouraging them to stoically endure knowing that they are not alone in such suffering. When He was suffering on the Cross of Calvary, our Lord Jesus lived this eighth Beatitude by forgiving His tormentors and praying for their forgiveness.

And when they had come to the place called Calvary, there they crucified Him, and the criminals, one on the right hand and the other on the left. Then Jesus said, "Father, forgive them, for they do not know what they do." And they divided His garments and cast lots.
Luke 23:33-34 (NKJV)

When we pause to allow the Holy Spirit to overhaul our lives with these teachings that begin with the Beatitudes, we embrace discipleship the way our Lord Jesus taught it. It was through these teachings that He raised 11 men that evangelized the entire humanity in their time. They are the foundations of a Christ-like life. Through these teachings, we are transformed daily into the nature of Christ. He invited each disciple and would-be disciple with these words in Matthew 11:28-30 (KJV):

Come unto me, all ye that labour and are heavy laden, and I will give you rest. Take my yoke upon you, and learn of me; for I am meek and lowly in heart: and ye shall find rest unto your souls. 30 For my yoke is easy, and my burden is light.

In Acts 11: 25-26, the Bible records that Paul and Barnabas taught discipleship classes for one year at Antioch. It was there that disciples of our Lord Jesus Christ were first called Christians.

"Then, Barnabas departed for Tarsus to seek Saul. And when he had found him, he brought him to Antioch. So it was that they assembled with the church for a whole year and taught a great many people. And the disciples were first called Christians in Antioch.

When we use the Beatitudes to overhaul our lives and that of new believers, we position them and us to embrace the rest of the Sermon on the Mount and other teachings of the Bible to fill the world with believers who walk daily in the footprints of our Lord and Saviour Jesus Christ.

Here is what our Lord Jesus Christ said in His conclusion of the Sermon on the Mount:

"Therefore, whoever hears this saying of mine and does them, I would liken him to a wise man who built his house on the rock. And the rain descended, and the floods came and the wind blew and beat on that house and it did not fall, for it was founded on the rock. But everyone who hears this saying of mine and does not do them, will be like a foolish man who built his house on the sand and the rain descended, and the floods came, and the wind blew and beat on that house and it fell and great was its fall".

- Matthew 7:24-27

Building Our Lives on the Rock

We build our lives on the rock when we live daily according to our Lord Jesus's teachings, rather than the philosophies of men or their pet theories. If our lives are to reveal the Light of Jesus that shines in the darkness of sin, ignorance, and evil, which the darkness cannot overcome, we must follow our Lord Jesus's teachings for all humanity. And there are advantages when we build our lives on His teachings.

The first advantage is the companionship of the Holy Spirit: *"But the Helper, the Holy Spirit whom the Father will send in My name, He will teach you all things and bring to your remembrance all things that I said to you" (John 14:26).*

The Holy Spirit is the actual Teacher. As He teaches us, He calls up learned principles of life from our Lord Jesus's life and teachings, as the circumstances demand.

The second benefit is the wholesome LAMINAR flow of our lives. The Lord's teachings can bring various aspects of life together in a beautiful blend that profoundly satisfies and fulfills us. Some have a business but no family; others have a family but no company, while others have a confused and complicated business, church, and family relationships. This chaotic state is the classic picture of the house that is built on sand.

The Sermon on the Mount

A brief word about the Sermon on the Mount, of which the Beatitudes constitute the beginning. These teaching are geared to produce the new creation in Christ who will shine the Light of Christ's life on the world around. When we read in 2nd Corinthians 5:17: *"When a man is in Christ he is a new creation, old things are passed away and*

behold all things have become new;" we see in the
Beatitudes the first steps in that transformation.
The Bible teaches that the mind of the new
believer in Christ must be renewed to enable him
to discover what is the acceptable and perfect
will of God. We find this in Romans 12:2,

*"And be not conformed to this world but be ye
transformed by the renewal of your mind, so that you
may prove what is that good, what is that acceptable,
and what is that perfect will of God",* in every
situation and every circumstance!

Our Lord and Saviour Jesus Christ, declared the
blessedness of changed lives who have become
new creatures in Christ. *"Oh! that blessedness of the
poor in spirit, for theirs is the kingdom of heaven."*
When seen in this context, the Beatitudes become
a present continuous experience, here on earth
rather than the pious hopes of heaven. The poor
in spirit have the foretaste of the Kingdom of

heaven here and now and will enjoy it in its fullness in the future heaven.

THIS IS WHY THE BEATITUDES MUST BE SEEN AS THE BEGINNING OF CHRIST'S MANUAL, FOR A KINGDOM LIFESTYLE HERE ON EARTH.

They take us into the vast world of heaven's Kingdom here on earth, particularly its practical relevance in every area of life. The reality of the Kingdom of heaven has a far-reaching implication spiritually, as we shall see subsequently.

CHAPTER 1

BLESSED ARE THE POOR IN SPIRIT

"Blessed are the poor in spirit, for theirs
is the kingdom of heaven."
- Matthew 5:3

The first Beatitude declares: *"Blessed are the poor in spirit"*. Who are the poor in spirit? What is the poverty of the spirit all about? This question is important to us because it promises a gain of a present, daily reality of the Kingdom of heaven. According to the Greek, the poverty here described is not the poverty of a man who works for a living but is poor, but the poverty of a man who is destitute and so can only wholly trust

God for sustenance. We have an example of this in Psalm 34:6:

"This poor man cried out and the Lord heard him and saved him out of all his troubles."

Again we have an example in Psalm 9:18:

"For the needy shall not always be forgotten, the expectation of the poor shall not perish forever."

So what then does spiritual poverty mean? Let me lift Barclay's thoughts on this again. **'Blessed are the poor in spirit'** means blessed is the man who has realized his utter helplessness and has put his whole trust in God. If a man realizes his total failure and has put his entire trust in God, two things that are opposite sides of the same thing will enter into his life.

- He will become completely detached from things, for he will know that things don't bring happiness or joy or security.

13

- He will become completely attached to God, for he will know that God alone can bring hope and strength and support.

This is where the overhaul takes place. The man who is poor in spirit has escaped the clutches of materialism and the deceit of worldly pleasures and goods to embrace the need of his soul to seek the LORD God Almighty to be a Light that is shining in the darkness rather than part of the darkness. This is the man who has realized that things mean nothing and that God means everything. This Beatitude is not about the good in material poverty as such a notion is absurd. By feeding the five thousand on one occasion and four thousand on another, our Lord Jesus alleviated need whenever the demand arose. He had compassion on the people and would not send them away hungry, lest they faint on the way. Material poverty is not a good thing. There is nothing blessed or to be happy about when people live in economic depression and poverty. Admittedly, the Christian gospel aims to eradicate that kind of poverty by giving men hope amid hopelessness, by empowering them through faith to trust God for a breakthrough in their lives. The poverty which is blessed is the poverty of spirit. Barclay summarizes it this way, *"When a man realizes his utter lack of resources to meet life and finds his help and strength in God."*

Now, to this man then, who has no confidence in himself and depends on God for everything, belongs the Kingdom of heaven's reality in this world. What is the Kingdom of heaven on earth? How do we understand this? Our Lord Jesus taught us that the coming of the Kingdom of God brings with it the doing of the will of God. So, the Kingdom of heaven exists for the man who pursues God's will and God's ways so that God's power will be released to usher in a different kind of life that brings great hope and joy. No matter who we are and where we are, we must come to God with this spirit of complete helplessness if we must experience the wonderful nature of His favour in life. I recall now what the Holy Spirit taught me some years ago.

I was asking the Lord in prayer to help me do something. Then, the Spirit of the Lord stopped me and said, "*Your prayer is good but not good enough. If I help you do this thing, I will be limited by what you can do even at its very best*". Then, He taught me that my prayer should be, "*Lord please come and do this in me and then do it through me,*" and He said to me, "*When I do it in you, and I do it through you then you will have a capacity that is beyond your natural ability.*"

When we, for example, begin to show sacrificial love, humility, and self-abasement beyond natural ability, we realize with time that the Kingdom of heaven has genuinely started to be manifest through our lives. We acknowledge in time that what our life portrays is the life of Christ by the power of the Holy Spirit, and that brings about this joy that defies description. The blessedness, joy, and deep satisfaction of the poor in spirit, is the reality of the Kingdom of God that has become his possession.

This is the revelation behind John 3:34.

"For He whom God has sent speaks the words of God, for God does not give the Spirit by measure; The Father loves the Son and has given all things into His hands."

Now, this scripture tells us that God was satisfied to leave all things in the hands of our Lord Jesus Christ because He received the full measure of the Spirit, and expressed the life in the spirit in its fullest measure. In other words, God released the fullness of the spirit so that our

Lord Jesus could manifest the fullness of life in the spirit. There is no loss of life in the spirit through our Lord Jesus. The overhaul is truly in place when we allow the Spirit of God to have His way in us and have His way through us: the overhaul is in place when we trust the strength the Holy Spirit gives rather than our own strength: the overhaul is truly established when we cast away our weaknesses to possess His strength in all situations. This is the way our Lord Jesus practised poverty of the spirit revealed to us in

John 5:19:

Then Jesus answered and said to them, most assuredly I say unto you the Son can do nothing, absolutely nothing of himself but what He sees the Father do, for whatever the Father does the Son also does in like manner".

When we understand and practice poverty of the spirit, we too will not try to do anything by ourselves, no matter the pressure, the gain, the loss, the threat of failure, the promise of reward or success, except what we see the Father do. This is what puts the endorsing voices from heaven in their perspectives, particularly the first voice which came after the baptism of our Lord Jesus Christ in Matthew 3:13-17:

"Then Jesus came from Galilee to John at the Jordan to be baptized by him and John tried to prevent Him saying, I need to be baptized by You and You are coming to me? But Jesus answered and said to him, "Permit it to be so now; for thus it is fitting for us to fulfill all righteousness; then He allowed him. When He had been baptized, Jesus came up immediately from the water and behold the heavens were open to him and he saw the spirit of God descending like a dove and alighting upon Him and suddenly a voice

19

came from heaven saying this is my beloved Son in whom I am well pleased". (NKJV)

Now John the Baptist tried to dissuade our Lord Jesus Christ from undergoing water baptism onto repentance. In John's opinion, it wasn't necessary. A man without the original sin does not need water baptism. But poverty of spirit kicked in when our Lord Jesus replied: *"I must fulfill all righteousness,"* which means I must let the Father have His way. Therefore, it must be so. Righteousness means standing wherever God is standing on any matter. That's how we fulfil all righteousness. This the true overhaul of our nature and character, when we defy pressure, opinions, advantages, losses, intimidating and threatening personalities and circumstances and stand where the Father stands or where God's word stands on any matter.

The voice from heaven registered the Father's delight and approval of His Son's way of life on earth: *"This is My beloved son in whom I am well pleased."* Now you and I can understand the basis of the endorsement.

- My beloved Son satisfies Me completely.

- My beloved Son does not hinder My Spirit.

- My beloved Son does not resist My will.

- I have full confidence in Him that He will yield to Me in all things and all the time.

This is what poverty of the spirit is all about.

We can see that poverty of the spirit may begin at the feeling of utter helplessness when we cling to God as the source of all things. It will then graduate to the level at which our Lord Jesus Christ practiced it, which says, "nothing is good except it is done the way God wants in detail." Blessed are the poor in spirit for theirs is the Kingdom of heaven here on earth. The poor in spirit can bring heaven down to earth in their lives, in their worlds as husbands, wives, doctors, nurses, lawyers, pastors, bishops, apostles, artisans, politicians, people in business, governors, presidents, judges anyone in any position in life anywhere.

This God-like permanent joy derives from the realization that in every area of our lives where we have attained the victory, our humanity is no longer hindering the divinity within us. The Christ-life is being expressed through us completely unhindered. What we realize is that we have to grow in this attribute of poverty of the spirit. Having seen the extent to which poverty of the spirit can take us in life, our first step must be to desire to live daily, albeit moment by moment, a life that reveals this poverty of the spirit. Our Lord Jesus expressed it in diverse ways. We have seen the one in Matthew 3: 14-15 where John tried to dissuade Him from water baptism.

The wonder of poverty of the spirit is that we are ready and willing to make whatever sacrifice is needed to reveal that God is supreme in our lives and that His will is our command. And this says nothing about the direction in which His will and His Word is taking us. God's will and His Word took our Lord Jesus to the Cross of Calvary to die for our sins. That struggle in the Garden of Gethsemane revealed how tough the choice can be:

Then He said to them, "My soul is exceedingly sorrowful, even to death. Stay here and watch with Me." *He went a little farther and fell on His face, and prayed, saying,* "O My Father, if it is possible, let this cup pass from Me; nevertheless, not as I will, but as You will." *Then He came to the disciples and found them asleep, and said to Peter,* "What? Could you not watch with Me one hour? Watch and pray, lest you enter into temptation. The spirit indeed is willing, but the flesh is

23

weak." *Again, a second time, He went away and prayed, saying,* "O My Father, if this cup cannot pass away from Me unless I drink it, Your will be done."
Matthew 26:38-42

We have these challenges all the time. Nobody knows how exactly God would want to lead us, what He would want to do through us. But poverty of the spirit ensures that we are willing and ready to follow wherever He leads. Therefore, our desire in prayer should be, *"Lord, please give me grace always to fulfil all righteousness so that Your purposes can come through unhindered through me and unhindered by me."*

Now we see another Scripture in John 6:38.

"For I have come down from heaven not to do my own will but the will of Him who sent Me."

The deep desire is not to be driven by men's applause and approval which is the world's measure of success, but exclusively by the Father's delight and command. This is how to reveal the higher level of poverty of the spirit when we accept that the ultimate good in time and eternity is not to manifest or establish God's will but in letting the divine will flow unhindered in our lives without regard to the outcome.

Think of when our Lord Jesus prayed in the Garden of Gethsemane. Perhaps, somebody would have said, "*If You die like a criminal, this finishes the whole purpose for which You came. Don't even dare, don't even try it, don't even...*" But our Lord Jesus kept saying, "The first question is, *how does God want His will accomplished? I would rather do what God wants to be done in the way He wants it done even at the risk of losing everything.*"

Here is an example in the life of our Lord Jesus Christ recorded in John 6:24.

"When the people, therefore, saw that Jesus was not there nor His disciples, they also got into boats and came to Capernaum, seeking Jesus and when they found Him on the other side of the sea they said to Him Rabbi! When did You come here?" Jesus answered them and said, "Most assuredly I say unto you, you seek Me, not because you saw the signs but because you ate of the loaves and were filled. Do not labour for the food which perishes, but for the food which endures to everlasting life, which the Son of man will give you because God the Father has set His seal on Him".

After He had fed five thousand men not counting women and children, a multitude reappeared at His meetings the very next day. They were determined to follow Him, and He saw their motives as they gathered around Him, and their numbers swelled. Our Lord Jesus was unimpressed by the numbers, and rather than cuddle them and organize them into a church of followers; He told them some hard truths about their desire to see Him. *"Your loyalty and determination are all about bread."*

The Bible says many of these followers went home. They never followed Him again. John 6: 65 records:

"And He said, "Therefore I have said to you that no one can come to Me unless it has been granted to him by My Father." From that time, many of His disciples went back and walked with Him no more. Then Jesus said to the twelve, "Do you also want to go away?" But Simon Peter answered Him, "Lord, to whom shall we go? You have the words of eternal life. Also we have come to believe and know that You are the Christ the Son of the living God".

In essence, our Lord Jesus had said to the thousands of disciples whose following was motivated by bread, "Hey, you guys! I'm sure you're here for another lunch or dinner. Listen, don't keep fighting for your belly; fight for the life that the Son of man is giving. I don't need any disciples except for the ones my Father brings. I don't need any disciples to massage My ego or to say how wonderful My preaching is. I don't need them to show how wonderful everything I am doing is. No! I only want the people that the Father has brought".

It was after this that He began to tell them about the need to eat the flesh of the Son of Man and drink His blood. When they heard that teaching the bread-inspired followers thought to themselves, *"We have heard enough. Now it's time to go home because this man wants to turn us into cannibals."* And He said it deliberately to sift the crowd and know those who were truly called to serve God in His kingdom on earth. Only twelve people persevered and followed our Lord Jesus. The rest went away. May you and I be amongst those who continue, learning the way of the kingdom, learning how poverty of the spirit can take us to great heights of blessedness in our lives so that God's kingdom and His purposes can be fulfilled in and through us. Bow your head and let us pray.

PRAYER

Blessed are the poor in spirit, for theirs is the Kingdom of God. Holy Spirit please show me where I am in living this virtue – poverty of spirit. Show me how to live and practice poverty of the spirit, so that the blessedness of the Kingdom of God on earth will be mine. Heavenly Father, may Your spirit purge my heart of everything that hinders God, His purpose, and will. May the attractions of fame and fortune not derail the Kingdom of God in my life. I yield to You to guide, instruct, and direct me so that I will lead and live just the way You want, following my master Jesus's footsteps. I thank You for hearing me. For in Jesus' precious name, I pray. Amen.

CHAPTER 2

BLESSED ARE THEY THAT MOURN
FOR THEY SHALL BE COMFORTED

Blessed are they that mourn, for they
shall be comforted
- Matthew 5:4

Our first task here is to understand this open-ended mourning. The Bible says in Isaiah 53:3:

"He is despised and rejected by men, a man of sorrows and acquainted with grief; and we hid as it were our faces from him, he was despised, and we did not esteem Him." (NKJV)

Our Lord Jesus Christ was a man of sorrows and acquainted with grief. In this Beatitude, He speaks to us about this blessedness associated with grief or sadness, which prepares and positions the soul for a fruitful life and an eternity with God. In the book of Ecclesiastes, King Solomon spoke of grief's benefits in reconstructing the mind and reordering our priorities. Ecclesiastes 7:2-4;

"Better to go to the house of mourning than to go to the house of feasting, for that is the end of all men and the living will take it to heart. Sorrow is better than laughter, for, by a sad countenance, the heart is made better. The heart of the wise is in the house of mourning, but the heart of fools is in the house of mirth." (NKJV)

When we take grief in its usual sense, we see that those who allow grief to reorder their priorities refocus their minds on eternal rather than temporal things. They also receive a depth of comfort by the Holy Spirit, which comes out of their grief. The Bible speaks of a weeping that may endure for a night before joy comes in the morning, as we read in Psalm 30:5. In the loss of loved ones, we are comforted by the hope of a reunion at Christ's appearing. Furthermore, the Scriptures teach us in 1 Thessalonians 4:13 not to grieve like those without hope.

Our Lord Jesus Christ was a man of sorrows. His sorrow embraces all grief but particularly the sadness resulting from the ravages of sin on man and his society. This Beatitude calls us to share in this grief so that hope and joy can come to those who mourn.

This Beatitude holds a special place in the overhaul of our lives and character. Men and women are known to indulge themselves in their sins and treat their failings with levity. But when we understand sorrow for sin, our attitude changes, and the many consequences of the evil we do, keep us in constant mourning and drives the effort to make changes.

In my nation Nigeria, we have quite a lot to grieve about in this area; the tragedy of missed opportunities due to the ravages of sin, covetousness, selfishness, and greed abound. We must mourn over the many ruined destinies arising from wickedness, selfishness, and insatiable desire and lust for gain. We must grieve over countless lives lost to corruption in diverse ways. This mourning is for communal sins of omission and commission that should galvanize change in our society, changes that build and protect lives.

Our Lord Jesus Christ was a man of sorrows, but His grief was not for His sins because He had none. It was for the tragedy of communal sins and rebellion against God, which retards spiritual progress and society's general welfare; and serves to steer it toward periodic disasters as revealed in Mathew 23:37-39.

"O Jerusalem, Jerusalem, the one who kills the prophets and stones those who are sent to her! I often wanted to gather your children together as a hen gathers her chicks under her wings, but you were not willing! See, your house is left to you desolate, for I say to you, you shall see me no more till you say, "Blessed is He who comes in the name of the LORD!" (NKJV)

We may talk glibly about communal sins but cannot truly grieve. We know that genuine and heartfelt grief can help us become God's answer to the masses' prayers for relief. The worst scenario is not just when we talk glibly about these evils but also when we tragically participate or spearhead them.

We move to the next grief, which is grieving for our sins. There are quite a few who would state that this is the major grieving that our Lord Jesus Christ had in mind in this Beatitude. We have ample examples of this in the Bible, notably King

David mourning for his sins against Uriah the Hittite, one of his most loyal servants. Here is a sample of his grief in Psalm 51:1-4:

"Have mercy upon me, O God, according to Your lovingkindness; According to the multitude of Your tender mercies, blot out my transgressions. Wash me thoroughly from my iniquity and cleanse me from my sin. For I acknowledge my transgressions, and my sins are ever before me. Against You, You only have I sinned, and done this evil in Your sight- That You may be found just when You speak and blameless when You judge." (NKJV)

Now, the Bible teaches that this is godly sorrow that leads to repentance. As we read in 2 Corinthians 7:8-10; The Apostle Paul said,

If I made you sad with my letter, I don't regret it, although I did regret it then. I see that the letter caused you sorrow, though only for a while. Now I'm happy, not because you had such sorrow, but because your sorrow led you to repentance. For you were sorry

in a godly way, and so you were not hurt by us in any way. For having sorrow in a godly way results in repentance that leads to salvation and leaves no regrets. But the sorrow of the world produces death. (ISV)

We must pause to understand the end of this kind of sorrow; the result is repentance. Repentance always produces change or a turnaround from evil. John the Baptist, in his preaching, calls that change the fruit of repentance. In Mathew 3:7-8, the Bible says: "But when John saw many Pharisees and Sadducees coming to where he was baptizing, he said to them, *"You children of the serpent, who warned you to flee from the coming wrath? Produce fruit that is consistent with repentance."* (ISV)

In understanding this fruit of repentance, we must also understand the distinction between attrition and contrition.

Attrition versus Contrition

Attrition is said to be when the constant fear of punishment keeps us from doing evil. It is similar to doing right because of the fear of penalties under the law.

Contrition, on the other hand, is a broken heart driven by grief and deep remorse as revealed in Psalm 51:16-17;

For you do not desire sacrifice or else I would give it. You do not delight in burnt offerings. The sacrifices of God are a broken spirit, a broken and a contrite heart; these O God, You would not despise. (NKJV)

Contrition or heartfelt repentance involves a deep conviction that usually leads to genuine change. We see true repentance in King David's life because we never heard about sexual immorality again after his sincere regret. The Apostle Paul articulated the cause of this sorrow.

It is a part of our struggle to keep sin away from our lives:

I know that nothing good lives in me, that is in my sinful nature, I want to do what is right, but I can't, I want to do what is good, but I don't. I don't want to do what is wrong, but I do it anyway. But if I do what I don't want to do, I'm not really the one doing wrong; it is sin living in me that does it. I have discovered this principle of life, that when I want to do what is right, I inevitably do what is wrong. I love God's Law with all my heart, but there is another power within me that is at war with my mind. This power makes me a slave to the sin that is still within me. O, what a miserable person I am, who will free me from this life that is dominated by sin and death? Thank God, the answer is in Jesus Christ, our Lord!
So you see how it is. In my mind I want to obey God's law, but because of my sinful nature, I am a slave to sin.
- Romans 7:18-25 NLT

Indeed, the answer to this grief is in Jesus Christ and the Comforter, the Holy Spirit, who provides us with the inner strength and power to have victory over temptations.

"Blessed are they that mourn for they shall be comforted." Herein lies the mystery of our victory over sin in this world. It is not usual to associate blessedness and joy with grief and sorrow. Still, we are told here that when change accompanies remorse and grief, the Holy Spirit restores hope and faith with love. The inner strength by which we overcome sin in our lives is released within us, bringing the blessedness of the joy of overcoming temptation in us.

For example, a family may be at the brink of disaster because of the father's sin or the mother's. Still, genuine repentance with contrition can restore relationships by healing the memories of past hurts and recreating a new beginning. Contrition or godly sorrow is the real evidence of repentance because such penitence brings restitution and change. Contrition of heart brings up a sincere desire to forsake the sin after the Spirit of Grace has mortified the flesh and released energy to our inner man to conquer the desire to do evil.

The prophet Isaiah captured the Father's delight with those who experience genuine sorrow for their sins:

For thus says the high and lofty One who inhabits eternity, whose name is Holy: I dwell in the high and holy place, and also with those who are contrite and humble in spirit, to revive the spirit of the humble, and to revive the heart of the contrite.
-Isaiah 57:15 (NRSV)

When you read the same Scripture in another translation, the thought becomes clearer:

"I am the high and holy God, who lives forever. I live in a high and holy place, but I also live with people who are humble and repentant, so that I can restore their confidence and hope.

-Isaiah 57:15 (TEV)

The Almighty God is so delighted by genuine repentance that the sinner is restored and uplifted to His side. The restoration gained through this response by the God of heaven and earth brings much joy to us. That joy also derives from the understanding that the victory over that particular sin, which looked unattainable hitherto, is achievable. Subsequently, the Holy Spirit sustains us in that victory because of the power He releases within us. King David showed us how the Holy Spirit used his contrition to work genuine change within him after the Prophet, Nathan, brought him the convicting word, *"You are the murderer!"*

He showed his grief in what he said to Nathan, "I have sinned against the Lord." Subsequently, we never heard that David messed with sexual immorality ever again. The Holy Spirit gave him victory. "Oh, how blessed are those who mourn for their sins," is to show the joy of overcoming temptations and sin.

The Apostle Peter speaking to the people after the healing of the disabled person by the Beautiful Gate said in Acts 3:19:

"Repent, therefore, and turn to God so that your sins may be wiped out. So that times of refreshing may come from the presence of the Lord, that He may send the Messiah appointed for you, that is Jesus who must remain in heaven till the time of universal restoration that God announced long ago through His Holy prophets."

Joy always comes to us when a turning towards God follows repentance. Sin belonging to the past departs, and times of refreshing, blessedness, and joy come to sustain us in godliness and truth.

Godly Sorrow and Besetting Sins

We need to understand Godly sorrow in dealing with besetting sins spoken about in Hebrews 12:1:

Wherefore seeing we also are compassed about with so great a cloud of witnesses, let us lay aside every weight, and the sin which doth so easily beset us, and let us run with patience the race that is set before us,
-Hebrews 12:1 (KJV)

One translation calls besetting sin the sin that clings so tightly to us. It has become so familiar that we have rationalized our indulgence in it and have even tried to justify it and defend our evil participation. And anytime such a thing happens to us, we have become slaves to the particular sin.

Sometimes, when we commit such evil, it falls on our blind spot. From anatomy, we learn that when an image falls on your blind spot, you never see it, even when people try to show you, and say to you, "*This thing you're doing is wrong,*" you wouldn't be able to see it. The reason is that your beclouded understanding is insensitive to the anger of God against that sin. So, it is important to look at the rest of that Scripture in Hebrews 12:1-4:

Wherefore, seeing we also are compassed about by so great a cloud of witnesses, let us lay aside every weight and the sin which could easily beset us and let us run with patience the race that is set before us — looking unto Jesus the author and finisher of our faith; who for the joy that was set before him, endured the cross, despising the shame and has sat down at the right hand of the throne of God. For consider Him that endured such contradiction of sin as against Himself, lest you be wearied and faint in your minds.

Besetting sins can ruin the new life that God has given to us in Christ Jesus. They make us hypocrites and make the world around us cynical about Christ's gift of new life that we profess. But when there is contrition or godly sorrow that leads to a conviction, there is a determination to search for and access the Holy Spirit's inner strength to crush the tempter's power in our lives. When victory over temptation is secured, we enter into that joy of a deeper kind. It is the joy that testifies that salvation and victory over sin are genuinely a part of our lives. And it is to us in this circumstance that our Lord Jesus said, "Blessed are they that mourn, for they shall be comforted." Contrition ensures that sin remains exceedingly sinful and repugnant to us as revealed in Romans 7:13:

Now, did something good bring me death? Of course not; rather, sin used something good to cause my death so that sin would be recognized as sin.

Through the commandments, sin becomes more sinful. And that's why when we find ourselves in a besetting sin, we must look in the mirror of God's word so that the sin can become exceedingly sinful. Once sin becomes exceedingly sinful to us, we are off to seek God's power to overcome it in our lives. The Lord allows us to see sin for what it is, something that must be dreadful to us because it makes God very angry and always brings His judgment over our lives. And if we're Christians, it opens the door for chastisement. Then there is the Holy Spirit's power to live out what grace did for us through Christ.

Now this new attitude to sin is the major overhaul of this Beatitude. It gives us the right mindset to what is wrong, and through the grief of realizing that we have been indulging in evil complacently, we awaken to a new life in Christ.

With this new attitude, we first embrace forgiveness through our Lord Jesus Christ's blood, shed on the Cross of Calvary. Secondly, the Holy Spirit's power is available to live the Christ-life, despite all the odds. In the same place of prayer, where we access our sins' forgiveness, we must also access the power and inner strength to lead godly lives daily. To emphasize our sins' forgiveness without the accompanying ability to lead holy lives is to preach an incomplete gospel. The Apostle prayed for inner strength to lead a new life in Christ for the Ephesian Christians:

For this reason, I kneel before the Father, from whom every family in heaven and on earth is named: I pray that He may grant you according to the riches of His Glory to be strengthened with power in your inner being through His Spirit and that Christ may dwell in your heart through faith. I pray that you may be rooted and firmly established in love, that you may be able to comprehend with all the saints, what is the length and width and height and depth of God's love

and to know Christ love that surpasses knowledge so that you may be filled with all the fullness of God.
- Ephesians 3:14-19 (CSB Bible)

When we have contrition and conviction, we pray for inner strength to walk daily in the twin love that sums up God's commandments: Love for God, which is obedience with reverence or fear, and love for man - a self-sacrificing love. Contrition, which registers our aversion to sin, ensures that we seek the Holy Spirit's wisdom and counsel to steer clear of temptations and compromised and compromising situations. Also, we seek His inner strength to resist every pressure to compromise with evil.

There is blessedness and joy that come to those who mourn for their sins. They arise from the daily victory over diverse temptations. When we allow Christ to dwell in our hearts by faith, the Holy Spirit can express Christ's character and power through our lives.

Attrition, which is repentance for fear of punishment, is more readily overcome by sin's pleasures and the pressures to compromise for one gain or benefit. Also, attrition is a calculated risk, which is of the head and not of the heart. It is a reasoning objection which has not yet seen the sin in its ugly sinfulness. When Joseph escaped the lustful overtures of Potipher's wife in Exodus chapter 39, he pointedly told the lady that what she was proposing was an act of wickedness. More importantly, it would be a sin against God. This Joseph's response is the correct attitude to sin that this Beatitude is recommending to us.

The Apostle Paul summarizes the new attitude of the believer overhauled through the blessedness of grief over sin:

See that no one renders evil for evil to anyone, but always pursue what is good both for yourselves and for all. Rejoice always, pray without ceasing, in

everything give thanks; for this is God's will in Christ Jesus for you. Do not quench the Spirit. Do not despise prophecies. Test all things; hold fast what is good. Abstain from every form of evil.
—*1 Thessalonians 5:15-22 (NKJV)*

In conclusion, our Lord Jesus Christ says to you, and I as His followers: "Blessed are they that mourn, for they shall be comforted."

Blessed are the people who grieve over communal sins and ask God to send deliverance to rescue society from their grip.

Blessed are those who grieve over their sins and ask God for power and inner strength to lead godly lives. David did that, and he never went into adultery again. So, to anyone and everyone who needs to experience victory over sin in any area of life, comes the word of our Lord Jesus Christ that says, "Blessed are they who mourn, for they shall be comforted."

PRAYER

Our Father in heaven, may it please You to grant us the grace to mourn over our sins and the communal sins around us. Please make us Your joyful instruments of righteousness where we are that Light may come to our world in darkness through us, in Jesus name we pray, Amen.

CHAPTER 3

BLESSED ARE THE MEEK

"Blessed are the meek for they shall inherit the earth."
- Matthew 5:5.

Our Lord Jesus Christ said of Himself, "I am meek and lowly in heart, and you will find rest for your souls." He extends an invitation to be conformed into His image and character to us: to be meek and lowly is to be like Him. To understand what the Lord Jesus was teaching here, we must have a firm grasp of what meekness is all about.

- Who are the meek?

- What is the character trait that is associated with meekness?

But before we go any further, we must make a mental note of the lessons from the first two Beatitudes.

The first Beatitude calls the poor in spirit blessed. It is an attitude we must adopt in our relationship with God. To inherit the kingdom of heaven, we need to consider ourselves utterly helpless outside of God's grace and mercy.

In the second Beatitude, we learned that those who mourn for their sins, and the communal sins around them would be comforted by God's forgiveness that brings God's peace that passes all human understanding. Those who know to grieve over their sins can sense the grief that the Almighty God feels over sin as recorded in Genesis chapter 6:

The LORD observed the extent of human wickedness on the earth, and he saw that everything they thought or imagined was consistently and totally evil. So the LORD was sorry he had ever made them and put them on the earth. It broke his heart.

Genesis 6:5-6 (NLT2)

It broke His heart indeed. When we realize what our sins do to our God, we enter into mourning because His commandments have made sin exceedingly sinful to us. Therefore, it follows that the meek must show this trait before God to merit a reward. So what does meekness before God represent in our relationship with Him and with our fellow man? Let us look at what saints of old thought about this. Here is Butler's context in his analytical Bible:

"It is nigh onto impossible to describe meekness with one word. We have used the word 'pliant', but that does not fully describe meekness though it seems involved in most actions of meekness.

Meekness is the condition of God's people in their respect of God and submission to God in contrast to the world that blasphemes God and rebels against God.

Meekness involves being mild and gentle, the attitude which prefers to bear injuries rather than return them.

Meekness consists of a pliant heart that wills to do the will of God. Meekness is not weakness or an easygoing disposition or even timidity; neither is it deficient in strength of purpose. It is a gentleness of strength of purpose.

It is not being weak and distraught. It is not a biological but a spiritual condition. It is not a henpecked husband or a browbeating wife or a yes-man on the job; that's not what meekness is about."

Now here's a similar thought from Saint Andrew's exposition:

"We have a tendency to think of meekness as synonymous with weakness. We think of the meek as personified by Caspar Milquetoast. Meekness seems to

describe someone who lacks a backbone, who has a vacancy of courage in his heart, but that is not what is meant by the biblical concept of meekness. It is a quality frequently manifested by exceedingly strong people who do not use their strength or power to crush others or to lay them low."

The prominent model of weakness in Old Testament times was Moses, yet we know that he was one of the most powerful men in human history from another perspective. He used his strength and the power that God gave him with gentleness.

There was one in the New Testament far stronger than Moses, even our Lord Jesus Christ Himself, and yet it was said of Jesus in the prophecy of Isaiah, that *a bruised reed He will not break* (Isaiah 42:3). We observe how our Lord Jesus dealt with the Pharisees and the Scribes, He responded to strength with strength, but when He encountered people who were broken and lonely because of their sin, our Lord Jesus ministered to them with gentleness. Our Lord Himself was a paragon of meekness, yet no one has ever mistaken our Lord Jesus for someone weak or spineless. Meekness, therefore, will represent those who have a great deal of strength but are characteristically gentle and controlled in the way they manifest their power. They are always using their strength when required, and with great humility, they never allow their strength to intimidate or crush the weak.

The meek show great resilience under pressure and their demeanor may belie their great strength and capacity to take suffering and pain without complaining. The meek are submitted to God's will, in God's way, and will pay whatever price is needed to ensure that God's purposes are accomplished. Humility is a vital expression of meekness because it is constantly looking up to God for approval and endorsement in the pursuit of the divine will and purposes on the earth. Meekness is, therefore, willing and ready to make itself of no reputation. That is the mind of Christ, who made Himself of no reputation or importance. Our Lord Jesus demonstrated humility by choice and not one imposed by force or circumstances.

Moses was very meek, but the secret was that God led him in all his moves and decisions. True meekness is the result of the constraints of God through the Holy Spirit. Practicing God's restraints in our daily lives is always valid evidence that our flesh has been crucified with Christ. When we refuse to retaliate, not out of weakness but out of restraint, we show that our meekness is from the Lord and His Holy Spirit. And it does not matter the perception of the world around us, even their mockery and disdain should not make us change course if we have true meekness from the Lord Jesus.

Meekness can be a tough act, particularly in an area where we have a lot of strength. The tendency is to shove people aside who appear to be weaker, shove them away and take over, leaving them with bruised egos and lowered self-esteem from which some may not recover. During His arrest in the Garden of Gethsemane, our Lord Jesus Christ showed great restraint in the exercise of His spiritual authority and power. We see this in Matthew 26:50-56.

Jesus said to him, (He was talking to Judas) "Friend, why have you come? Then they came and laid hands on Jesus and took Him. And suddenly, one of those who were with Jesus stretched out his hand, drew his sword struck the servant of the High Priest, and cut off his ear; But Jesus said to him, put your sword in its place for all who take the sword will perish by the sword.

Or do you think that I cannot now pray to My Father, and He will provide Me with more than twelve legions of angels? But how then could the Scriptures be fulfilled, that it must happen this way?

In that hour, Jesus said to the multitude, "Have you come out as against a Rabi, with swords and clubs to take Me? I sat daily with you teaching in the temple, and you did not seize Me." But all this was done that the Scripture of the prophet might be fulfilled. Then all the disciples forsook Him and fled. (NKJV)

Now, notice that our Lord Jesus Christ still found the inner strength to call Judas His betrayer, friend, because what was happening was in God's perfect will. Through meekness, He showed incredible inner strength in the face of great adversity. Meekness enables us to be angry for the right reasons and not for the wrong reasons, as revealed by our Lord Jesus Christ Himself in Mark 3:1-6.

And He entered the synagogue again, and a man was there who had a withered hand. So they watched Him closely whether He would heal him on the Sabbath so that they might accuse Him. And He said to the man who had the withered hand, "Step forward." Then He said to them, "Is it lawful on the Sabbath to do good or to do evil to save life or to kill?" But they kept silent and when He had looked around at them in anger, being grieved by the hardness of their hearts, He said to the man, "Stretch out your hand," and he stretched it out, and his hand was restored as whole as the other. Then the Pharisees went out immediately and began to plot with the Herodians against Him, how they might destroy Him. (NKJV)

Our Lord Jesus Christ did not permit anger for the wrong reason, nor did He allow the misuse of power and authority as played out in Luke 9:51-56:

When the days drew near for Him to be taken up, He set His face to go to Jerusalem. And He sent messengers ahead of Him, who went and entered a village of the Samaritans, to make preparations for Him. But the people did not receive Him, because His face was set toward Jerusalem. And when His disciples James and John saw it, they said, "Lord, do you want us to tell fire to come down from heaven and consume them?" But He turned and rebuked them. And they went on to another village. (NRSV)

James and John thought it outrageous that someone with so much power and authority could be disrespected without the offender's suffering consequences. How dare these Samaritans refuse to receive our Lord Jesus? They needed to be taught a lesson! But our Lord Jesus said to them, "Oh no, we never do things that way." When we curse and threaten because we are not getting our way or because we suffer injustice or a bypass of our rights and privileges, we must admit that we lack His meekness. His anger was never against personal injustice, but against evil, against injustices by the morally bankrupt and hypocritical self-righteous.

You and I will admit that we need a significant overhaul in our understanding and practice of His depth of meekness. To be angry for the right reasons and never angry for the wrong reasons, particularly when it comes to personal slight and disrespect, is a new height to reach for each of us. To never misuse or abuse our strength, especially when it confers a great advantage, is a new maturity level.

Now, what is the reward for meekness? The meek shall inherit the earth. Here again, there is some difficulty in understanding this reward. Look at other opinions on this, the first being Saint Andrew's Commentary:

"The promise given to those who are meek is that they will inherit the earth. When someone dies and a will is read, the deceased's heirs discover the contents of the estate that has been left to them. The heirs are excited to find out that the family home or the family farm will pass into their hands. However, in terms of the

vastness of this earth, such parcels are small. The inheritance in this Beatitude is the whole earth. We are told that we are heirs of God and joint heirs with Christ, all things in the world have been given to our Lord Jesus Christ and the redemption He brings is not simply for the sins of people, but for a falling planet. At the present time the whole creation groans together, waiting for the redemption of the sons of God. But at the consummation of His kingdom, the Lord will usher in a new Heaven and a new earth. And that new heaven and new earth will be the inheritance of the meek."

Now from John Wesley, we read:

"The meek shall inherit the earth. They shall have all things really necessary for life and godliness. They shall enjoy whatever portion God has given to them here on this earth, now and then, hereafter, they shall possess the new earth wherein dwelt righteousness."

The word, inheritance, will suggest something that can only happen after the demise of the testator who wrote the will. Our Lord Jesus Christ promised us the gift of the Holy Spirit, but only after His glorification:

In the last day, that great day of the feast, Jesus stood and cried, saying, "If any man thirsts, let him come unto Me and drink. He that believeth on Me, as the Scripture hath said, out of his belly shall flow rivers of living water. But this spake He of the Spirit, which they that believe on Him should receive: for the Holy Ghost was not yet given; because that Jesus was not yet glorified.
- John 7:37-39 (KJV)

The Holy Spirit is the one that produces diverse rivers of living water to provide abundant life for God's children through faith in Christ, as revealed in the words of our Lord Jesus in John 10:9-10.

"I am the door. If anyone enters by Me, he will be saved, and will go in and out and find pasture. The thief does not come except to steal, and to kill, and to

destroy. I have come that they may have life and that they may have it more abundantly." (NKJV)

So there is every reason to believe that the meek shall inherit the earth. This includes the earth that now is, and by consensus, the world that is to come. To inherit the world or earth now is to possess the abundant life promised by our Lord Jesus Christ in John 10:10. The indwelling Holy Spirit will create opportunities on the path of our pursuit of the divine purpose to meet our needs and give us this promised abundant life. The Psalmist had this together in Psalm 37:3-11.

Trust in the Lord and do good; then you will live safely in the land and prosper. Take delight in the Lord, and He will give you your heart's desires. Commit everything you do to the Lord, Trust Him, and He will help you. He will make your innocence radiate like the dawn, and the justice of your cause will shine like the noonday sun. Be still in the presence of the LORD, and wait patiently for Him to act. Don't worry about evil people who prosper, or fret about their wicked schemes. Stop being angry! Turn from your rage! Do not lose your temper — it only leads to harm. For the wicked will be destroyed, but those who trust in the LORD will possess the land. Soon the wicked will disappear; though you look for them, they will be gone. The meek will possess the land and will live in peace and prosperity. (NLT2)

Of greater significance beyond the present earth, as mentioned earlier, is the promise of a new heaven and a new earth revealed in 2 Peter 3:13.

Nevertheless, we according to His promise look for a new heaven and a new earth wherein dwell righteousness. Wherefore beloved, seeing that you look for such things, be diligent that you may be found of Him in peace without spot and blameless. (NKJV)

This new heaven and earth is the righteous's final home, where we shall live with God forever in our eternal home, worshiping and serving Him forever. 'Blessed are the meek for they shall inherit the earth' is an incentivized Beatitude. It encourages us to put on meekness like the Lord Jesus Christ and see how it enables us to prosper the Kingdom of God through our lives and reap the fruit of our labour in this life and life that is to come. Now, here are some encouraging Scriptures on meekness that empower us to inherit the earth now and in the world to come.

Seek the Lord all ye meek of the earth, who have upheld His justice, seek righteousness, seek humility; it may be that you will be hidden in the day of the Lord's anger.
- Zephaniah 2:3(KJV)

In other words, Zephaniah the prophet was saying, meekness can lead to divine protection and bring us under the shadow of His wings, for they that dwell in the secret place of the Most High shall abide under the shadow of the Almighty. In Luke 6:27-31, the Scripture says:

But I say to you who hear, love your enemies, do good to those who hate you, bless those who curse you, and pray for those who spitefully use you. To him who strikes you on the one cheek, offer the other also, and from him who takes your cloak, do not withhold your tunic either. Give to everyone who asks of you. And from him who takes away your goods, do not ask them back, and just as you want men to do to you, you also do to them likewise. (NKJV)

The Lord Jesus here shows us how to deal with our horizontal relationships with other men so that our Father in heaven will be pleased with us and give us blessings on the earth because of our obedience. In 1 Corinthians 6:6-7, the Bible says:

But brother goes to law against brother, and that before unbelievers; Now, therefore, it is already an utter failure for you that you go to law against one another. Why do you not rather accept wrong? Why do you not rather let yourselves be cheated? (NKJV)

Here, the Apostle Paul admonished the Church to bear wrong, rather than take the matter to court. And he admonishes us to walk in the Spirit so that God will bless us. Finally, in Galatians 5:22-23, the Bible says,

But the fruit of the Spirit is love, joy, peace, longsuffering, gentleness, goodness, faith, meekness, temperance against such there is no law. (KJV)

And it is for this reason that the Bible says in Galatians 6:1,

If a man be overtaken in a fault, you who are spiritual, restore such person in the spirit of meekness, considering yourself, lest you also be tempted. (KJV)

PRAYER

O thou Spirit of the living God, who dwells in my heart, I yield to You this moment to grow the virtue of meekness in my heart in the pattern of my Lord and Saviour, Jesus Christ, so that His meekness can be manifest through my life. Please help me not hinder You in the exercise of meekness, and grant this my heart's desire for I pray in the precious name of Jesus. Amen.

CHAPTER 4

BLESSED ARE THEY THAT HUNGER
AND THIRST FOR RIGHTEOUSNESS

Blessed are those who hunger and thirst for
righteousness, for they shall be filled.
- Mathew 5:6

In a sense, the fourth Beatitude is a follow-up on the first three. In the first Beatitude, we learn that poverty of the spirit positions us to enter the Kingdom of heaven. When we lie prostrate before God, confessing that we have no hope of eternal life, except through His grace and the pardon we receive for our sins through the blood of Jesus His Son, then, the gates into the Kingdom of God are opened to us. The Spirit of the living God comes to indwell us to reveal Christ in us and through us.

In the second Beatitude, we come to the man who is deeply sorrowful for his sins. Having come into the Kingdom of God, he is wounded by his errors because he realizes that it is his sins that drove our Lord Jesus to suffer such a gruesome death that made Him a criminal by association. When his sins deeply grieve him, the Holy Spirit comes to comfort him with the assurance of salvation and the cleansing power in the blood of Jesus, provided by our Father in heaven.

In the third Beatitude, we meet the meek, the humble: his high sense of indebtedness to our Saviour comes from the fact that our Lord Jesus came from heaven in humility to die for our sins. The meek follow in our Lord Jesus Christ's footsteps and inspired and impacted by His meekness, strive daily to follow in His steps.

And now we have come to the fourth Beatitude, which is going in a slightly different direction. Having been forgiven of every sin, having mourned for the past and present sins with the brokenness that teaches humility, the fourth Beatitude challenges us to hunger and thirst for righteousness in line with God's truth and His ways.

Now, let us focus on this hunger and thirst. We must understand the depth to which this desire should go. By using very familiar passions to describe this Beatitude, our Lord Jesus Christ revealed the turnaround of a new life in Christ, the bold initiatives of the soul born into the Kingdom of God. Consider the hunger. This hunger is not the hunger of a man who wants to top up before his next meal, but the deep hunger of a starving man desperate for food.

It is not the gentle hunger that a little sandwich will quench, but the desperate need of a starving man who must eat or face death. When we come to the thirst, our Lord Jesus did not talk about the thirst that a cup of tea or a glass of cold water can satisfy. The picture is that of a desert traveler whose throat has been parched by the sand storms and must get to the next oasis to find water or die of thirst.

This hunger and thirst for righteousness have great intensity, depth, and desperation. This longing is for the righteousness of thought and action or nothing. The next thing involved in this text is that it is hunger and thirst for righteousness in every area of life and not just in some areas. This calls for further explanation. Theologians tell us that the tense used here in the Greek, for righteousness depicts the man who has dedicated his entire life to the pursuit of wholesome righteousness in every area of life. Also, this is not the hunger and thirst of the man who is willing to do the right or be on the right now and again: *This is the hunger and thirst of the man who wants to get it right always.* He is determined to do the right thing at every turn, act the right way, and respond with the right attitude. Even when he fails, this intense desire never leaves him. He continues to press on till help comes to him to give him the inner strength and courage to succeed and be satisfied.

It is important to note that our Lord Jesus Christ was not talking about the man who has attained perfection in righteous living, no matter the circumstance and no matter the situation. Instead, our Lord was talking about the man who, despite his failings oft-repeated, is not discouraged but is hungry and thirsty for what is right to know it and do it no matter where and when, and no matter how much it costs him. Our Lord Jesus is saying that those in whom exists these depths of hunger and thirst for righteousness will be satisfied; they will have a deep sense of accomplishment. This satisfaction is deep within, a witness in their soul that the life they are living on earth is compatible with their citizenship of heaven.

This Beatitude is where we encounter a very significant overhaul in our character. We are familiar with doing the right thing now and again. But this insatiable desire to get it right always and still strive to get it right after several failings is life-transforming.

The reward is that they will be satisfied! Here, we see that the God of heaven is looking not just at the results of our efforts but the intensity of our desire to get it right and to do the right thing by God and man no matter the cost. And this is an intensity that will not wax and wane, but one that is as consistent as it is persistent. The fourth Beatitude is considered by many as the most demanding Beatitude. It reveals how much we understand the demands of our new life in Christ.

What is the result of this hunger and thirst for righteousness? The first thing it shows is that we have a deep understanding of our citizenship in the Kingdom of Heaven. This understanding revealed in 2 Corinthians 5:17, says:

Therefore, if any man be in Christ, he is a new creation; old things have passed away, behold all things have become new. (NKJV)

Old things must pass away, and all things must become new. We can see this hunger and thirst in a Christian who is always quick to ask, *"Is this the way a Christian should respond in this situation?"* They consistently search for what is right before God, and once they find it, they commit themselves to do it. As disciples of our Lord Jesus Christ, we enter into this hunger and thirst for righteousness in our spheres of influence or duty. Our delight is to see right prevail over wrong all the time. The Apostle Paul had this to say to them about this deep, heartfelt turnaround of the new man in Christ:

This I say, therefore, and testify in the Lord, that you should no longer walk as the rest of the Gentiles walk in the futility of their mind.
- Ephesians 4:17(KJV)

In other words, Paul is saying in this verse that there is a new life a citizen of the Kingdom of Heaven lives daily, which is distinct from the old ways and different from the way unbelievers live. It is a travesty for a Kingdom citizen to live and act like unbelievers.

Having their understanding darkened, being alienated from the life of God because of the ignorance that is in them, because of the blindness of their heart.
–Ephesians 4:18(KJV)

So, what exactly is he saying here? Anyone whose life is unchanged after becoming a citizen of the Kingdom of heaven is utterly ignorant of Christ's way of life. Their understanding is still corrupted by lusts and by all manners of sin.

Who being past feeling have given themselves over to lewdness, to walk all uncleanness with greediness.
- Ephesians 4:19 {KJV)

Here, the Apostle says that those who do not pursue righteousness lack this driving spiritual sensitivity that creates and sustains this deep hunger and thirst for righteousness.

But you have not so learned Christ.
– Ephesians 4:20 (KJV)

In other words, anyone buried in sins, covetousness, and greed has not understood this fourth Beatitude of Christ. It teaches that blessedness exists for those in the Kingdom of heaven, who have a deep insatiable hunger and thirst for righteousness.

If indeed you have heard Him and have been taught by Him as the truth is in Jesus
- Ephesians 4:11(KJV)

We should pay particular attention to the notion of being taught by Christ; that's why we are talking about making disciples the Jesus way and the Beatitudes as the overhauling kit used to achieve it. This is the singular most important reason we must make disciples the Jesus way, using His spiritual tools. We must fulfill that part of the Great Commission that says we must teach new believers in Christ to observe all things that our Lord Jesus has commanded us.

Our Lord's voice must be repeated in the ears and hearts of new believers so that an insatiable hunger and thirst for righteousness will grow in their innermost being, whether they be rich or poor, educated or illiterate, born with a silver spoon or born poor. This hunger and thirst for righteousness have no barrier of status, social class, or attainment in life. The billionaire and the pauper must have this insatiable hunger for righteousness. This is the truth that is in our Lord Jesus. This is what He taught. We cannot and must not teach otherwise, or we will stand condemned by His words in *Ephesians 4:22*.

"That you put off concerning your former conduct the old man, which grows corrupt according to deceitful lusts."

There are always, and always would be, the deceitful lusts that put gain over godliness, pleasure over sacrifice, and does not admit self-denial in the pursuit of righteousness. Here, we learn to discard the old laissez-faire approach that is ready to accommodate all kinds of corruption and vice in the pursuit of gain and replace it with an insatiable, persisting hunger and thirst for righteousness.

And be renewed in the spirit of your mind
-Ephesians 4:23 (KJV)

To be renewed in the spirit of our minds is to change the way we think, and begin the new and vital search for the good, the acceptable and perfect will of God spoken about in Romans 12:2;

"And do not be conformed to this world, but be transformed by the renewing of your mind, that you may prove what is that good, and acceptable, and perfect will of God." (NKJV)

From Ephesians 4:24, we learn to *put on the new man, created according to God in true righteousness and holiness.* This new citizen of the Kingdom of Heaven was created according to God in true righteousness and holiness. The early apostles made disciples the Jesus way by teaching them to observe everything He commanded.

The next to be revealed in this hunger and thirst is that citizens of the Kingdom of God not only get rid of their iniquity and purge themselves of every work of unrighteousness, but they also must pursue righteousness, anywhere and everywhere. What God is looking to see to release the Spirit of righteousness on our people and nation are men and women who sincerely desire to see righteousness enthroned in their lives and society. Besides, they are working and choosing all of the righteousness anytime, anywhere. The Spirit of righteousness provides the quickening power always to do it right and continue seeking to do it right even after repeated failures.

Prophet Hosea has a word in Hosea 10:12,

Sow for yourselves righteousness, reap in mercy, break up your fallow ground, for it is time to seek the Lord till He comes and rains righteousness on you. (NKJV)

It is necessary to look at how the early fathers of faith saw this Beatitude, those who laboured diligently in centuries past to ensure that the truth of God's Word is not lost. We begin with Chromatius. He taught that we must seek after righteousness with earnest desire, not with faint-hearted energy. Indeed, he calls those persons 'the blessed' who search for righteousness and virtually burn with passionate longing in their hunger and thirst. For if each one of us hungers and thirsts for righteousness with eager desire, we can do nothing else but think and seek after righteousness. It is necessary then that we eagerly desire that for which we hunger and thirst.

We move on to Saint Chrysostom. He says: "Note how drastically our Lord Jesus expresses it, for Jesus does not say 'blessed are those who cling to righteousness,' but 'blessed are those who hunger and thirst after righteousness,' not in a superficial way but pursuing it with their entire desire. By contrast, covetousness's most characteristic feature is a strong desire to get more and more even when there is no need. Our Lord Jesus urged us to transfer this desire, this covetousness for a new object to freedom from greed, and deep hunger for righteousness."

Apollinaris: *"When Luke mentioned these blessed ones, he called them simply, 'those who hunger,' but Mathew defines them as those who willingly and from a longing for the good, abstain from fleshly pleasures. Both Luke and Matthew speak similarly; whoever longs for God's righteousness has found what is truly desirable."*

By joining thirst to hunger, we see desire lumped with a burning passion for realization described as a thirst. By the craving of thirst, our Lord intends to indicate the heat and burning of intense longing. He says that such a person will be filled or satisfied. But such fulfillment does not produce a turning away but rather an intensification of the desire.

Here is another observation by an unknown author: *"To hunger and thirst for righteousness is to desire God's righteousness."* People should hear and do God's righteousness not as though they hear and do it unwillingly but from their heart's desire. Every good we do must be done out of this sort of love for righteousness, or it will not please God.

We can see why the Lord, through John the Apostle, was not calling everyone to drink, but only those thirsty, saying, *"If anyone thirsts, let that one come to Me and drink."* Similarly, it was not of nothing that He spoke of those who hunger and thirst for righteousness. Whoever desires or craves for righteousness wants to live actively according to God's righteousness. This is proper for the person with a good heart. One who thirsts for righteousness wants to acquire the knowledge of God. That, one can gain only by studying the Scriptures. This is the fitting attitude of the person with an attentive and hungry heart, for they shall be satisfied, or be filled with the abundance of God's reward. Greater is the Lord's reward than even the happiest desires of the saints."

Now, let us try and bring all these ancient opinions on this together. We can see that the early fathers emphasized the knowledge of God's righteousness from the Scriptures. And when we discover it, we must entertain a persistent longing to live by it continually. Notice that Saint Chrysostom said it is the opposite of covetousness. He pointed out that rather than fill our hearts with desires to acquire more and more things, we should rechannel such energy and desire to walk in righteousness.

Anywhere corruption is said to be endemic, we can immediately see that the cure is for God's saints to develop a deep and insatiable hunger for righteousness to God's glory and the common good. All manner of evil, be they at home, at work, or in Church, have their solution in this pursuit of practical righteousness according to God's word. The Father in heaven has vested His saints with Christ's righteousness to enable them to enter His family and enter the Kingdom of God.

Our Lord Jesus Christ says that as saints then, we must nurse and entertain an insatiable hunger for righteousness to manifest the very life of Christ, which is the light that enlightens every soul that comes into the word.

THROUGH THIS INSATIABLE PURSUIT OF RIGHTEOUSNESS, WE WILL PRODUCE HIS LIGHT THAT SHINES IN THE DARKNESS AND WHICH THE DARKNESS CANNOT OVERCOME.

The Apostle Paul had this in mind when he wrote to the Philippians in Philippians 2:12-16,

Therefore my beloved, as you have always obeyed, not as in my presence only but now much more in my absence, work out your own salvation with fear and trembling. For it is God who works in you both to will and to do of His good pleasure. Do all this without complaining and disputing. That you may become blameless and harmless children of God without fault in the midst of a crooked and perverse generation among whom you shine as light in the world, holding fast the word of life so that I may rejoice in the day of Christ that I have not run or laboured in vain. (NKJV)

As ministers of the word of life, you and I must think further ahead to the day we shall be called to appear before Christ's judgment seat. Will He approve of the work we did in His name? Will there be a record of the souls that we led to pursue God's righteousness in the world? The

Apostle Paul was deeply concerned that unless the Philippians lived their lives in righteousness by shining as a light in a crooked and perverse generation, all his labour and work among them would have been in vain.

Undoubtedly, such a scenario will be a monumental tragedy. That we produced men and women who are attending Church, paying their tithes and offerings, and sponsoring various charities: But, we couldn't produce men and women that lead godly lives on the earth, men and women who shrink from covetousness and greed. As St. Chrysostom said, we must make disciples the Jesus way to protect our labour before Him on that Day of Judgment. This is why we must teach the people of God that our Lord said that those who have entered the Kingdom of Heaven must have an insatiable hunger and thirst for God's righteousness on earth.

Now let's go to the reward, *'Blessed are those who hunger and thirst after righteousness, for they shall be filled.'* What exactly does it mean to be filled or to be satisfied?

Sow for yourself righteousness, reap in mercy, break up your fallow ground for it is time to seek the Lord till He comes and rains righteousness on you.
- Hosea 10:12 (KJV)

The hunger and thirst for righteousness will lead us as Kingdom citizens, to sow righteousness like a seed anywhere and everywhere. This is imperative, for we reap what we sow. When we sow righteousness, the mercy of the Lord God Almighty will overtake us in multiple dimensions.

The next thing is to break up our fallow ground, which is to allow the Holy Spirit to soften our hearts to receive the truth of the Word of God, digest it and soon produce in us this insatiable hunger and thirst for righteousness everywhere we are in the world. It is time to seek the Lord, but for what? For the revival rain of righteousness that sweeps evil away and causes the light that is our Lord Jesus Christ's very life, to shine through our lives. To be filled then is to see our Father in Heaven empower us for righteous living that can bring about a revival of godliness. Spiritual empowerment makes us defiant and bold to stand for righteousness, no matter the threat, no matter the cost, no matter the pressure.

That is the satisfaction when we now sit back and say, 'Oh Lord, thank You. You prevailed through me. I did not prevail; God prevailed through me. He sent a clear word that enabled me to take the stance I took'.

Our Lord Jesus teaches us that this hunger and thirst for righteousness brings satisfaction because the Lord God Almighty rains righteousness from above by His Holy Spirit.

Note this, when the Holy Spirit comes down, He brings *conviction,* which is sorrow for sin, and then *conversion,* which is change - that is the satisfaction. You can see people's lives transformed; people who used to enjoy doing evil now turn around with the Holy Spirit's conviction and embrace change with joy and gratitude.

Conviction is similar to what happened on the Day of Pentecost after Peter preached. The Bible said that the people were pricked in their hearts and began to cry out, *'Men and brethren, what shall we do*?' Only the Holy Spirit can produce that, and when He does, it is genuine and leads invariably to the transformation of life and character. It is only by the Holy Spirit's power that you and I can practice a no-nonsense pursuit of righteousness in the world, to cause a revolution in morality, justice, and integrity that can transform our planet just the way He did before.

Religious Misconceptions

- **Doctrinaire religion** talks about worshipping and praising, but without the power to change lives, just mouthing the Bible without the ability to transform lives. Here is what the Bible says about this in Paul's letter to Timothy:

holding to the outward form of godliness but denying its power. Avoid them!
2 Timothy 3:5 (NRSV)

- **Marketing religion** is all about the benefits of belonging to Christ.

And wrangling among those who are depraved in mind and bereft of the truth, imagining that godliness is a means of gain.
1 Timothy 6:5 (NRSV)

- **Existential belief** just there to make my life better, that's all.

For those who live according to the flesh set their minds on the things of the flesh, but those who live according to the Spirit set their minds on the things of the Spirit.

Romans 8:5 (NRSV)

Our faith and religion will be meaningless unless they can produce in us this insatiable hunger and thirst for righteousness so that heaven can invade the earth with the Spirit of Holiness, which Hosea the prophet called the rain of righteousness. By the Spirit of Holiness, the practice of righteousness is made possible in the world through empowerment. It is time to seek the Lord till He comes and rains righteousness upon us.

Let us ask God to fill our hearts with this burning desire to work righteousness upon the earth. Our

Lord Jesus taught this in the fourth Beatitude, "Oh, blessed are they who hunger and thirst after righteousness, for they shall be filled." Let us then see the conclusion of the matter, in Titus 2:11-14:

For the grace of God has appeared, bringing salvation to all people.

It trains us to reject godless ways and worldly desires and to live self-controlled, upright, and godly lives in the present age, as we wait for the happy fulfillment of our hope in the glorious appearing of our great God and Savior, Jesus Christ.

He gave himself for us to set us free from every kind of lawlessness and to purify for himself a people who are truly his, who are eager to do good.

Titus 2:11-14 (NET)

A people zealous for good works is a people with deep, insatiable hunger and thirst for righteousness.

This is not something for the other person; this is something for you and me. Do I have this deep, insatiable hunger and thirst for righteousness at home, in my family relationships? Do I have it at work, in my business relationships? Do I have it in Church, sincere and truthful as it is in Christ?

The only way to have it is to go before the Lord and say, *"O Lord my God, you have taken me into Your Kingdom; please give me a deep hunger and an insatiable thirst for righteousness according to the teaching of this fourth Beatitude."*

PRAYER

LORD, please give us who pray, this insatiable hunger and thirst for righteousness that the Kingdom of God will flourish within us and prosper through our lives. Give us the courage and the boldness to stand firm and true to Your Word, in Jesus name we pray, Amen.

CHAPTER 5

BLESSED ARE THE MERCIFUL

Blessed are the merciful, for they shall obtain mercy.
- Matthew 5:7

First, we must understand the true meaning of the word *'Mercy.'* According to Practical Word Studies, it means to show kindness, compassion, benevolence, and forgiveness. Still from Practical Word Studies, we learn that mercy, in its practical application, means to have a forgiving spirit and a compassionate heart. And James 2:13 (Amplified) states that "judgment is without mercy to the one who has shown no mercy, for mercy triumphs over judgment."

Mercy is being kind and benevolent. It forgives those who are wrong, yet it is much more. It is empathy; it is getting right inside the person and feeling his emotion along with him; it is a deliberate effort, an act of the will to understand the person and his need through forgiveness. It is the opposite of being hard, unforgiving, and unfeeling. God forgives all those who forgive others. Understand then what our Lord Jesus Christ said because He presented mercy as a seed. This 5th Beatitude is the first Beatitude where you will reap what you sow - Blessed are the merciful for they shall obtain mercy.

In Genesis 8:22, after the flood, God made a covenant with humanity through Noah, and in that covenant, He said, *"While the earth remains, seedtime and harvest shall not cease."* And in Galatians 6, the Bible extended the boundaries of this eternal law of sowing and reaping beyond agriculture.

Do not be deceived; God is not mocked; for whatsoever a man sows, that he will also reap. For he who sows to his flesh, will of his flesh reap corruption, but he who sows to the Spirit will of the Spirit reap everlasting life.
- Galatians 6:7 (NKJV)

And then in verses 9 and 10 it says,

And let us not grow weary while doing good for in due season we shall reap if we do not lose heart. Therefore, as we have opportunity, let us do good to all, especially to those who are of the household of faith.

It is clear from the Scriptures that the eternal law of sowing and reaping applies to mercy, as revealed in this fifth Beatitude. The Lord Jesus Christ also explained this in His teaching on prayer in Matthew 6:12 - 15).

And forgive us our debts, As we forgive our debtors. And do not lead us into temptation, But deliver us from the evil one. For Yours is the kingdom and the power and the glory forever. Amen. "For if you forgive men their trespasses, your heavenly Father will also forgive you. But if you do not forgive men their trespasses, neither will your Father forgive your trespasses. (NKJV)

Mercy is reciprocal as we read earlier from James 2:13, 'For judgment is without mercy to the one who has shown no mercy.' Mercy triumphs over judgment.

God's Covenant of Mercy

When Moses asked to know God's ways and to see His glory, His spiritual ambitions caused the LORDd to reveal His nature. We see this in Exodus 34:5-7.

Now the LORD descended in the cloud and stood with him there, and proclaimed the name of the LORD. And the LORD passed before him and proclaimed, "The LORD, the LORD God, merciful and gracious, longsuffering, and abounding in goodness and truth, keeping mercy for thousands, forgiving iniquity and transgression and sin, by no means clearing the guilty, visiting the iniquity of the fathers upon the children and the children's children to the third and the fourth generation."

It is, therefore, necessary to understand the power of applying God's mercy in intercession. This knowledge of the truth that it is in God's nature to show mercy empowered Moses in his prayer of intercession for Israel after they rejected Joshua and Caleb's good report and preferred the other ten spies' evil report. Here is the prayer of Moses in part from Numbers 14:15-19 (TEV).

Now if You kill all Your people, the nations who have heard of Your fame will say that You killed Your people in the wilderness because you could not bring them into the land You promised to give them.

So now, LORD, I pray, show us your power, and do what you promised when you said, 'I, the LORD, am not easily angered, and I show great love and faithfulness and forgive sin and rebellion. Yet I will not fail to punish children and grandchildren to the third and fourth generation for the sins of their parents.' And now, LORD, according to the greatness of your unchanging love, forgive, I pray, the sin of these people, just as you have forgiven them ever since they left Egypt."

Moses took God's very words and presented them to Him in prayer. It invoked the right response. *"Pardon the iniquity of these people I pray, according to the greatness of Your mercy, just as You have forgiven this people from Egypt even until now."* Here, Moses revealed that we must deploy the knowledge of God's character gained in the study of the Bible when we appear before Him in prayer to desire His favour and compassion. We should learn to trust God's nature of mercy, forgiveness, and compassion and so stand on solid ground before Him. The God we serve is a covenant-making and a covenant-keeping God. Therefore, He demands that those who receive covenant mercy should show the same to their brethren.

In the same vein, David kept his heart of compassion for the descendants of Saul. We find this recorded in 2 Samuel 9:1 (TEV).

One day, David asked, "Is there anyone left of Saul's family? If there is, I would like to show him kindness for Jonathan's sake."

And then in verse 7 of the same chapter:

"Don't be afraid," David replied. "I will be kind to you for the sake of your father, Jonathan. I will give you back all the land that belonged to your grandfather Saul, and you will always be welcome at my table."

King David's response is the kind of response expected of those who receive covenant mercy. If you and I can go to God and say to Him, "Lord, You are a God of mercy, You show forgiveness and compassion. Please look upon me with compassion have mercy upon me." And then, the God of compassion visits us, answers our prayer, favours, blesses, and heals us: The Lord Jesus is saying to us, "*Go and do the same, for blessed are the merciful, for they shall obtain mercy.*" We continually sow seeds for our future needs when we show mercy, and these seeds show up like harvest in usual and unusual times of need. God looks upon all that we have sown and then favours us with a yield of mercy, which is always higher than what we showed. God's mercy shown to man requires the man to show compassion in return to his fellow man. Israel learned this in their covenant relationship with God.

GOD'S PATIENCE AND LONG-SUFFERING WITH THE SINNER IS DESIGNED TO GIVE HIM TIME AND SPACE FOR REPENTANCE.

The Apostle Peter acknowledged this in 2 Peter 3:8-9 (TEV).

But do not forget one thing, my dear friends! There is no difference in the Lord's sight between one day and a thousand years; to Him, the two are the same.
The Lord is not slow to do what He has promised, as some think. Inst ead, He is patient with you, because He does not want anyone to be destroyed, but wants all to turn away from their sins.

And because God's mercy is indispensable to life, we must be careful to understand it and live our lives daily according to its demands. Here are a few things we learn about the mercy of God in the Bible.

God's mercy is a product of His sovereign grace

There is no obligation on God to show mercy. His mercy is due to sovereign grace, which is after the counsel of His own will as revealed in Ephesians 1:11 (TEV):

"All things are done according to God's plan and decision, and God chose us to be his own people in union with Christ because of his own purpose, based on what he had decided from the very beginning."

1. God's covenant of love and mercy is deep and extensive

This depth was revealed to Moses on Mount Sinai and corroborated by the prophets, but it is never indulgent of sin. Mercy is shown to the repentant and not to the rebellious or disobedient.

"For one brief moment, I left you; with deep love, I will take you back.

I turned away angry for only a moment, but I will show you, my love, forever." So says the LORD who saves you.

"In the time of Noah, I promised never again to flood the earth. Now I promise not to be angry with you again; I will not reprimand or punish you.

The mountains and hills may crumble, but my love for you will never end; I will keep my promise of peace forever." So says the LORD who loves you.

Isaiah 54:7-10 (TEV)

Do you see the reason why He was angry for a season? It was because of their disobedience and persistence in sin. However, the moment they showed repentance, His anger turned to mercy, forgiveness, and compassion. It is unbelievable how quickly God's wrath turns to forgiveness when we are repentant. And that's what we need to understand from this 4th Beatitude, "Blessed are the merciful."

Those who receive God's covenant mercy need to develop this capacity to show mercy to those who offend them in the same manner as our God. We must be careful to understand God's covenant mercy. Sin will always make God angry and cause Him to chastise us if we persist and do not repent. Recalcitrance will cause God's anger to endure, as revealed in Isaiah 9:13-17 (TEV).

The people of Israel have not repented; even though the LORD Almighty has punished them, they have not returned to Him.

In a single day, the LORD will punish Israel's leaders and its people; He will cut them off, head and tail.

The old and honourable men are the head – and the tail is the prophets whose teachings are lies!

Those who lead these people have misled them and totally confused them.

And so the Lord will not let any of the young men escape, and He will not show pity on any of the widows and orphans, because all the people are godless and wicked and everything they say is evil. Yet, even so, the LORD's anger will not be ended, but His hand will still be stretched out to punish.

When there is rebellion, persistence in sin, and gross disobedience, the prophet reveals that God will have no choice but to turn His mercy to anger and judgment. His hand stretched out to judge can only be withdrawn by genuine repentance, as revealed in Psalm 25:4-11 (TEV).

Teach me Your ways, O LORD; make them known to me.
Teach me to live according to Your truth, for You are my God, who saves me. I always trust in You.
Remember, O LORD, Your kindness and constant love, which You have shown from long ago.
Forgive the sins and errors of my youth. In Your constant love and goodness, remember me, LORD!
Because the LORD is righteous and good, He teaches sinners the path they should follow.

He leads the humble in the right way and teaches them His will.

With faithfulness and love, He leads all who keep His covenant and obey His commands.

Keep your promise, LORD, and forgive my sins, for they are many.

The penitent learns to have confidence in God's mercy because God's nature is to show mercy to the repentant.

"According to their deeds, accordingly He will repay, fury to His adversaries, recompense to His enemies. The coastlands He will fully repay, so shall they fear the name of the LORD from the west, and His glory from the rising of the sun; when the enemy comes in like a flood, the Spirit of the LORD will lift up a standard against him. The Redeemer will come to Zion, and to those who turn from transgression in Jacob, says the LORD."

- Isaiah 59:18-20 (NKJV)

Yes! There is the judgment for the unrepentant, the disobedient, and the rebellious, but the Redeemer will come to Zion. He will come only for those who are repentant and turn away from their transgressions. King David showed us how to walk in the mercy of God. After he murdered Uriah, King David knew that the only way to regain favour with the LORD was genuine repentance, and he revealed this in Psalm 51:1-4.

"Have mercy upon me, O God, according to Your lovingkindness; according to the multitude of Your tender mercies, blot out my transgressions. Wash me thoroughly from my iniquity, and cleanse me from my sin. For I acknowledge my transgressions, and my sin is always before me. Against You, You only, have I sinned, and done this evil in Your sight – That You may be found just when You speak, and blameless when You judge."
- Psalm 51:1-4 (NKJV)

We need to know that God is merciful. He shows mercy, alright, but He waits for the sinner to repent before He does so. Now those who presume on God and then continue to live in sin, claiming that the God they serve is merciful, are self-deluded. God wants the sinner first, to repent.

In the book of Genesis, Joseph showed that he understood God's mercy and forgiveness in his dealing with his brothers. His brothers sold him into slavery, and then, Joseph went through a period of tough times and finally rose to become Prime Minister in Egypt in a season preceding a global famine. Joseph rose because he interpreted Pharaoh's dream that spoke about an impending famine. When the famine struck, there was abundance in Egypt, and so, his brothers came to buy corn for their families. By then, he had transformed into a distinguished and influential authority figure, far from the dreamy teenager they had sold to slave traders. He recognized them immediately he saw them, but they didn't recognize him. However, he did not show himself by acknowledging them as his brothers. He waited to observe the state of their hearts. He heard them speaking in Hebrew, which they did not know he understood.

Reuben, the eldest, said to them, "Listen, what is happening to us is because we sold our brother. I advised you then not to sell him. Look at us now; look at what has befallen us." They did not realize that Joseph understood every word they were speaking.

We see that his once envious and evil brothers had become repentant and broken. Then, Joseph revealed himself to them. He showed them compassion and mercy and forgave them. He restored their status of brotherhood and turned to be a blessing to them.

This Beatitude is about showing mercy. It is a major overhaul because it is in our nature to retaliate and revenge when we are badly treated. Our Lord Jesus is urging us, His disciples, to become like our God in being ready to show mercy to the repentant. We must forgive those who hurt us before we know that they are repentant, just like Joseph. He had come to terms with God's purpose in his ordeal before his brothers appeared before him.

After their father's death, Joseph's brothers said, "What if Joseph still hates us and plans to pay us back for all the harm we did to him?"

So they sent a message to Joseph: "Before our father died, he told us to ask you, 'Please forgive the crime your brothers committed when they wronged you.' Now please forgive us the wrong that we, the servants of your father's God, have done." Joseph cried when he received this message. Then his brothers themselves came and bowed down before him. "Here we are before you as your slaves," they said. But Joseph said to them, "Don't be afraid; I can't put myself in God's place. You plotted evil against me, but God turned it into good, in order to preserve the lives of many people who are alive today because of what happened.

You have nothing to fear. I will take care of you and your children." So he reassured them with kind words that touched their hearts.

-Genesis 50:15-21 (TEV)

Like Joseph, we excel in mercy when we forgive even before the offender is willing and ready to show repentance. Joseph had forgiven his brothers before he met them because he saw what the LORD did for him through their treachery when He promoted him from prison to palace. But Joseph did not throw mercy at the unrepentant; that will be like casting your pearls before swine or dogs. They will trample on it. There is no need to offer forgiveness to people that will not appreciate it. You forgive them in your heart and maintain a posture of readiness to receive them. But you should always allow them to come to repentance so that they value and appreciate and become grateful for mercy.

In genuine repentance then, we must acknowledge God's justice. God is right in judging us for our sins so we can plead for His mercy. Subsequently, we must rise to walk in righteousness and truth to avoid further judgment. It is essential to understand the way mercy and compassion work from God's perspective. This is, so we learn to practice acts of kindness His way.

- First, we must forgive because God is always willing to forgive us.

- Then we must give room for repentance for the offender.

- We must avoid indulging the sinner.

I remember a gentleman once said to his employer after he did something wrong (and both were Christians). He said: "When somebody does something wrong, you are supposed to forgive him." And his employer testified that when he said that, the Spirit of God said to him, "That's presumption. You should punish him."

Mercy is not for the self-indulgent who are inclined to take kindness for granted and keep doing what is wrong. This is why we must always trust in God's mercy when we appear before Him and be careful to truly repent of our sins and walk in His ways so that His mercy will gain forgiveness and restoration for us as revealed in the testimony in Psalm 66:16-20.

Come and hear, all you who fear God, And I will declare what He has done for my soul. I cried to Him with my mouth, And He was extolled with my tongue. If I regard iniquity in my heart, The Lord will not hear. But certainly, God has heard me; He has attended to the voice of my prayer. Blessed be God, Who has not turned away my prayer, nor His mercy from me! (NKJV)

The Psalmist said, "*I have a testimony!*" And what was his testimony? "*I went the wrong way, and I prayed to God for mercy, and He answered me. He had mercy on me.*" That's a remarkable testimony. Those who trivialize their sins or persist in iniquity trusting in God's mercy are inviting His chastisement. We are to approach the LORD in humility and genuine repentance that commits to walk in His ways and His fear all our lives. That's what Psalm 25:14-18 reveals to us.

The secret of the Lord is with those who fear Him, And He will show them His covenant. My eyes are ever toward the Lord, For He shall pluck my feet out of the net. Turn Yourself to me, and have mercy on me, For I am desolate and afflicted. The troubles of my heart have enlarged; Bring me out of my distresses!

Look on my affliction and my pain, And forgive all my sins.

Iniquity is always the cause of chastisement because God is a Holy God. Some people say presumptuously: "Well, in the New Testament, there is so much forgiveness and mercy." There is no difference between God's forgiveness and mercy revealed in the Old Testament, from that shown in the New. God has not changed. He has always forgiven and still forgives the repentant sinner.

Bless the Lord, O my soul; And all that is within me, bless His holy name!
Bless the Lord, O my soul, And forget not all His benefits:
Who forgives all your iniquities, Who heals all your diseases,
Who redeems your life from destruction, Who crowns you with lovingkindness and tender mercies
- Psalm 103:1-4 (NKJV)

God's Mercy in the New Testament

There is always this suggestion, which I mentioned earlier, that the God of mercy of the Old Testament is different from the God of mercy of the New Testament. Those who teach that are guilty of fatal error because they imply that God has changed. The immutability of the true God is clearly stated in Malachi 3:6-7.

For I am the LORD, I do not change; Therefore, you are not consumed, O sons of Jacob. Yet from the days of your fathers you have gone away from My ordinances and have not kept them. Return to Me, and I will return to you," says the LORD of hosts.

If God has not changed, and the God of the Old Testament is still the God of the New Testament, what has changed between the Old Testament and the New Testament? The way of atonement has changed. In the Old Testament, the blood of bulls and goats made atonement for sins, and this atonement was merely substitutionary. That is why the blood of animals only provides a covering for sin.

And whatever man of the house of Israel, or of the strangers who dwell among you, who eats any blood, I will set My face against that person who eats blood and will cut him off from among his people. For the life of the flesh is in the blood, and I have given it to you upon the altar to make atonement for your souls; for it is the blood that makes atonement for the soul.' Therefore I said to the children of Israel, 'No one among you shall eat blood, nor shall any stranger who dwells among you eat blood.'
- Leviticus 17:10-11 (NKJV)

In the New Testament, however, the blood of Jesus Christ does not just provide a covering for sin, but it purges the conscience and opens the heart for the Holy Spirit's indwelling presence.

For if when we were enemies we were reconciled to God through the death of His Son, much more, having been reconciled, we shall be saved by His life. And not only that, but we also rejoice in God through our Lord Jesus Christ, through whom we have now received the reconciliation.

-Romans 5:10-11(NKJV)

Now we received the atonement or reconciliation, and our conscience was also purged of iniquity as revealed in Hebrews 9:11-14 (KJV).

But Christ being come an high priest of good things to come, by a greater and more perfect tabernacle, not made with hands, that is to say, not of this building; Neither by the blood of goats and calves, but by His own blood He entered in once into the holy place, having obtained eternal redemption for us. For if the blood of bulls and of goats, and the ashes of an heifer sprinkling the unclean, sanctifieth to the purifying of the flesh: How much more shall the blood of Christ, who through the eternal Spirit offered Himself without spot to God, purge your conscience from dead works to serve the living God?

Forgiveness of sin by God's mercy shown to us through Christ Jesus, our Lord, and Saviour, is followed by the empowerment to lead godly lives. It is the Holy Spirit that leads us to walk in obedience, in truth, and righteousness before our God. This is the essence of the Apostles John's clear teaching in 1 John 3:4-10 (TEV):

4 Whoever sins is guilty of breaking God's law, because sin is a breaking of the law.

5 You know that Christ appeared in order to take away sins, and that there is no sin in him.

6 So everyone who lives in union with Christ does not continue to sin; but whoever continues to sin has never seen him or known him.

7 Let no one deceive you, my children! Whoever does what is right is righteous, just as Christ is righteous.

8 Whoever continues to sin belongs to the devil, because the devil has sinned from the very beginning.

The Son of God appeared for this very reason, to destroy what the devil had done.

9 Those who are children of God do not continue to sin, for God's very nature is in them; and because God is their Father, they cannot continue to sin.

10 Here is the clear difference between God's children and the devil's children: those who do not do what is right or do not love others are not God's children.

What the Apostle John is saying to us is that there are only two spiritual families. We have the children of God who practice righteousness because they have been born of God, His Spirit is in them, and the children of the devil who continue to sin and refuse to repent. So it's essential to understand that nobody can continue to sin and continue to plead God's mercy. The mercy of God is for the repentant.

Back to the fifth Beatitude, 'Blessed are the merciful for they shall obtain mercy.' The most incredible mercy we have received is the full salvation that came to us through Christ.

But God, who is rich in mercy, for His great love wherewith He loved us, Even when we were dead in sins, hath quickened us together with Christ, (by grace ye are saved); And hath raised us up together, and made us sit together in heavenly places in Christ Jesus:

That in the ages to come, He might show the exceeding riches of His grace in His kindness toward us through Christ Jesus.

- Ephesians 2: 4-7(KJV)

How do we obtain this mercy? It says, 'For by grace you have been saved through faith and that not of yourselves it is the gift of God not of works lest anyone should boast.' Grace brings us salvation, full and free, but the Holy Spirit in the same vein is given to us to empower us to live godly lives. We must not emphasize one without the other. Apostle Paul in writing to Titus, in Titus 2:11, said,

"For the grace of God that brings salvation has appeared to all men."

And what is that grace doing? It *teaches us that denying ungodliness and worldly lust, we should live soberly, righteously, and godly in this present age.* The balance must be there. Grace is full and free; every soul that repents, every soul that receives Jesus Christ as Lord and Saviour, no matter their past sins, is forgiven. But then, when they receive the Holy Spirit, they begin to manifest the character of Christ. And that's why God said in His original intent that we have to be transformed into the image of Christ not to become indulgent sinners who continue to plead for God's mercy.

Now what the Lord is saying in this fifth Beatitude is that those who have received so much mercy through Christ must be careful to show mercy themselves or risk losing God's mercy. He taught us this in Matthew 18:32-35 (NKJV).

Then his master, after he had called him, said to him, 'You wicked servant! I forgave you all that debt because you begged me. Should you not also have had compassion on your fellow servant, just as I had pity on you?' And his master was angry and delivered him to the torturers until he should pay all that was due to him.

"So My heavenly Father also will do to you if each of you, from his heart, does not forgive his brother his trespasses."

So, the Lord teaches us that recipients of the untold and unmerited favour and mercy of God must show mercy. This is also clear from Mark 11: 25-26.

"And whenever you stand praying, if you have anything against anyone, forgive him, that your

Father in heaven may also forgive you your trespasses. But if you do not forgive, neither will your Father in heaven forgive your trespasses." (NKJV)

It is clear that recipients of mercy, particularly those who have received salvation full and free, are blessed to show mercy to others.

A Look at the Compassion of Our Lord Jesus Christ

Compassion is a seed which we must sow in our horizontal relationship with our fellow men, and we are to show it in these diverse ways:

1. Compassion shown in intercession for the needs of others: The sick, the oppressed, the needy, the prisoners of conscience like Leah Sharibu and several others as revealed in Hebrews 13:1-3.

Let brotherly love continue. Do not forget to entertain strangers, for by so doing, some have unwittingly entertained angels. Remember the prisoners as if chained with them – those who are mistreated – since you yourselves are in the body also.

The Bible has a special place for the needy in 1 John 3:16-18, the Bible says:

By this, we know love, because He laid down His life for us. And we also ought to lay down our lives for the brethren. But whoever has this world's goods, and sees his brother in need, and shuts up his heart from him, how does the love of God abide in him? My little children, let us not love in word or in tongue, but in deed and in truth. (NKJV)

The Bible is saying to us, let our love, our compassion, benevolence, and forgiveness - be practical. We must remember that the poor have a special place in God's heart, as revealed in the Scripture below:

When you give to the poor, it is like lending to the LORD, and the LORD will pay you back.
- Proverbs 19:17 (TEV)

"One who augments wealth by exorbitant interest gathers it for another who is kind to the poor".
- Proverbs 28:8 (NRSV)

We must have what the Bible calls 'Bowels of Mercy and Compassion.' We are not called to meet the needs of the entire world, but just the needs of those that God brings our way.

2. Compassion shown as forgiveness of personal wrongs: This is revealed in Luke 17:3-4.

Take heed to yourselves. If your brother sins against you, rebuke him; and if he repents, forgive him. And if he sins against you seven times in a day, and seven times in a day returns to you, saying, 'I repent,' you shall forgive him." (NKJV)

Our Lord Jesus Christ did not recommend forgiveness for the unrepentant. You forgive him in your heart because the Bible says, *'while we were yet sinners, while we were rebellious against God, while we were still enemies of God, He forgave us.'* But God held His forgiveness until we came with repentant hearts to acknowledge the Saviour who died for our sins. Only then did He release His forgiveness to us and then sent the Holy Spirit to reassure us that we have become God's children.

3. Compassion shown as forgiveness of debts:

As part of showing mercy, God encourages us to receive grace to forgive those who owe us and cannot afford to pay their debts.

"When he began the reckoning one who owed him 10,000 talents was brought to him and as he could not pay, his lord ordered him to be sold together with his wife and children and all his possessions and payment to be made. So the slave fell on his knees before him saying have patience with me and I will pay you everything. And out of pity for him the Lord of that servant released him and forgave him the debt".
- Matthew 18:24 (NRSV)

The slave could not afford to pay, so his master forgave him. That is the lesson.

4. Compassion shown as benevolence to orphans and widows:

In the Book of Ruth, a wealthy man, Boaz, showed kindness to Ruth, a poor Moabitess, and a widow. Boaz had no ulterior motive of marriage or personal gain at this point. To him, Ruth was the widow who returned to Bethlehem with Naomi, her elderly mother-in-law, to support and care for her.

"At mealtime, Boaz said to her come here and eat some of this bread and deep your morsel in the sour wine, so she sat beside the reapers. And he heaped up for her some patch grain she ate until she was satisfied and she had some leftover. When she got up to glean, Boaz instructed his young man let her glean even amongst the standing sheaves and do not reproach her, you must also pull out some handfuls for her from

the bundles and leave them for her to glean and do not rebuke her".

- Ruth 2:14-16 (NRSV)

Boaz showed her compassion by instructing his staff to act beyond Israel's tradition, which said it was customary according to the law to reap your field and leave the corners for the poor and the widows. Boaz said, *'Not just the corners, but deliberately drop some harvest to the ground for her to collect so that she can have enough to share with her mother-in-law.'* So we must understand mercy and benevolence to people around us.

5. The compassion that overlooks wrongs done to us:

You know it's not everything we must fight over, as revealed in Proverbs 19:11, *"Those with good sense are slow to anger, and it is to his glory to overlook an offence."* We are not to become so sensitive as to view everything as an offence. We are not to be quarrelsome and irritable, always complaining and fighting about every little thing. No! The Scripture says it is to your glory to overlook what people do to you. When we fail to overlook offences, stress, and distress in families prevail because we have not learned to show mercy, ignore wrongs, and forgive without fuss.

These are the realities of our calling in Christ because if God were to regard iniquity, the Bible says, nobody will survive. Part of our showing mercy is to overlook so many wrongs and let peace and love prevail.

6. Compassion as seeds of generosity and kindness:

It is crucial to have a generous spirit.

"There is one who scatters, yet increases more; and there is one who withholds more than is right, but it

*leads to poverty. The generous soul will be made rich,
and he who waters will also be watered himself".*
- Proverbs 11:24(NKJV)

God is not calling us to be Father Christmas, but He calls us to meet needs as led by His Spirit, so that we don't go beyond the grace that we have. It is so important to understand this.

Now, we also have to understand the Father's forgiveness for His prodigal son. Hurts and pains within the family can run deep and may result in unforgiveness. The Father's love and mercy to the prodigal son teach us that we must ask for the grace to forgive.

"But when he came to himself, he said, 'How many of my father's hired servants have bread enough and to spare, and I perish with hunger! I will arise and go to my father, and will say to him, "Father, I have sinned against heaven and before you, and I am no longer worthy to be called your son. Make me like one of your hired servants."'

"And he arose and came to his father. But when he was still a great way off, his father saw him and had compassion, and ran and fell on his neck and kissed him."

- *Luke 15:17 (NKJV)*

Looking at the prodigal son's story as told by our Lord Jesus Christ, we immediately see that the Father's forgiveness restored the son's dignity. Even though the son was ready to be made a servant, the Father's forgiveness restored him fully to sonship. And that is what God is teaching us in this 5th Beatitude. When we show mercy, when we forgive those who have hurt us, we don't forgive them and then leave them cringing before us or groveling in the dust. No! In showing mercy, we forgive them, restore their dignity, restore their place, and restore the relationship to its normal state before the issues arose. Therefore, we must understand mercy from God's perspective so that we can respond like Him.

One of the greatest stories of mercy in the New Testament is the story of the Good Samaritan's compassion.

But a certain Samaritan, as he journeyed, came where he was. And when he saw him, he had compassion. So he went to him and bandaged his wounds, pouring on oil and wine; and he set him on his own animal, brought him to an inn, and took care of him. On the next day, when he departed, he took out two denarii, gave them to the innkeeper, and said to him, 'Take care of him; and whatever more you spend, when I come again, I will repay you.'
- Luke 10:33-35 (NKJV)

Now the Good Samaritan's story is very evocative. It drives us to examine our motives. The Jews and the Samaritans were not friends at all. However, there was a Samaritan, doing good to someone who was supposed to be his enemy.

The Bible says *he pitied him because he too was a traveler, perhaps.* That's why mercy is said to be empathy. You enter into the state of the man. The Samaritan must have said to himself, *'It could have been me because I travel this road too.'* Like our Lord Jesus said, *'whatsoever you would that men do to you, do even so to them,'* he felt prompted to act in this manner. So he went over, took care of the hurt man, paid his bills, and offered to pay more without even knowing him. That's a great example of the compassion of our Lord.

The friends of the person with paralysis show another story of compassion. The paralytic's friends overcame every obstacle to bring him to our Lord Jesus for healing.

So many gathered around that there was no longer room for them, not even in front of the door; and he was speaking the word to them. Then some people came, bringing to him a paralyzed man, carried by four of them. And when they could not bring him to

Jesus because of the crowd, they removed the roof above him; and after having dug through it, they let down the mat on which the paralytic lay. When Jesus saw their faith, he said to the paralytic, "Son, your sins are forgiven."

- Mark 2:2-5 (NRSV)

This story reveals compassion that goes all the way to assist the needy. You and I have received help from people. Perhaps, you went to an office, and you were desperate to get paid, and somebody went out of their way to find your file, and you were so grateful. But then, you didn't conclude your process or application that day, and you returned the next day, and then you saw the same person, and you said, *"Oh, thank you very much for your assistance yesterday. Thank God I met you here today. You know, I am not yet done with processing that my paper."*

And the person responds in a rather cold manner, *"Please, I'm not here to be helping you. I just helped yesterday."* That is the way we are sometimes. We help, show compassion and empathy, but only some of the way.

However, not the friends of the person with paralysis; these friends brought him to the Lord Jesus. They looked right, they looked left, and there was no way they could enter the place where the Lord was. Now, that house was not theirs, and so when they removed the roof and dug through it, they probably knew they would have to fix it, but I'm sure that wasn't even part of their thoughts. They knew that whatever it would take, they must bring this man to the Lord Jesus. Therefore, they went out of their way, removed the roof, and brought him down; then, our Lord Jesus forgave his sins and brought him back to health. That is why we can say this was not convenient compassion, but compassion determined to overcome every obstacle to get help for a friend.

7. Compassion as a sacrifice of time and resources with great forbearance: The Lord Jesus taught sacrificial living and tolerance, which is instructive for how we respond to provocation and human need in our relationships and interaction with people. He changed the practice of paying evil for evil.

"You have heard that it was said, 'An eye for an eye and a tooth for a tooth.' But I tell you not to resist an evil person. But whoever slaps you on your right cheek, turn the other to him also. If anyone wants to sue you and take away your tunic, let him have your cloak also. And whoever compels you to go one mile, go with him two. Give to him who asks you, and from him who wants to borrow from you do not turn away. - Matthew 5: 38 – 42 (NKJV)

And let us not grow weary while doing good, for in due season we shall reap if we do not lose heart. Therefore, as we have opportunity, let us do good to all, especially to those who are of the household of faith.

- Galatians 6:9-10 (NKJV)

It is essential to understand that we have received so much mercy from God, and He obligates us to show mercy. That's the way we continue to sow the seed of mercy and compassion in our lives.

PRAYER

Heavenly Father, O for the grace to show mercy to all the people around us, show kindness, show love and care, go the extra mile, be benevolent and sacrificial – May the grace to do these be released into our lives. As many as are born of the Spirit of God, as many as know you as Saviour and Lord, O God, grant us grace to show mercy, that we may continue to receive mercy in our lives. If there is unforgiveness in our hearts, we receive grace to show mercy and to forgive so that the Spirit of the living God will bear fruit in our lives. We thank You, O Lord our God because grace is being given to us to show mercy. We receive that grace, and thank you, for it, in Jesus' name, we pray. Amen.

CHAPTER 6

BLESSED ARE THE PURE IN HEART

Blessed are the pure in heart, For they shall see God.
- Matthew 5:8

This sixth Beatitude is the most challenging because it addresses the highest need in man's heart, which is to behold the excellence of his Creator. Moses desired this with all of his being when he said to the Lord God Almighty in Exodus 33:18, *"Show me Your glory."* God said to him, *'If I dare show you My glory, the glory of My face Moses, you will be consumed by it.'*

However, we observe in Scripture that the twenty-four elders surrounding the throne of God in heaven do not wear face masks like the angels. The Bible says in Revelations 4:4, '*Around the throne were twenty-four thrones, and on those thrones, I saw twenty-four elders sitting, clothed in white robes, and they had crowns of gold on their heads*,' and they had no covers on their faces. But of angels, it was said in Isaiah 6:2-3, '*Above it stood seraphim; each one had six wings: with two he covered his face, with two he covered his feet, and with two he flew. And one cried to another and said: Holy, holy, holy is the Lord of hosts; the whole earth is full of His glory!*'

Because man is of higher creational hierarchy than angels, a fully sanctified man represented by the four and twenty elders surrounding the throne is allowed to behold God. This Beatitude is not about eternity. It is not about the sanctified saints who are already in heaven, but about here and now. Blessed are the pure in heart 'now,' for they shall see God.

As one commentator said, the problem of seeing God is not a deficiency in our optic nerve but a deficiency in the purity of our heart. Therefore, there is a beholding of God to which our Lord Jesus Christ is inviting you and me. A beholding that is here and now and not in eternity. While you and I pass through time, we can behold God in the excellence of His Glory. We can enter into the heavenly bliss, that transcendental happiness for those who live daily in the shadow of the Almighty.

It behooves us, therefore, to study this Beatitude carefully. It calls us to behold God and experience life in the shadow of His glory on earth. If we can have Mount Hermon's transcendental experience where our Lord Jesus Christ experienced transfiguration in His full glory, our lives would never be the same again. So, what exactly is "purity of heart?" Here are some examples that suggest the meaning:

The Greek word is '*Katharos*.' It describes purity, as seen in metallurgy. Silver, gold, and diamond are so purified that every trace of impurity is removed, allowing the precious metal to dazzle in magnificent beauty. *Katharos* also means unmixed purity, natural like pure wool, pure cotton, not a mixture of sixty percent wool, forty percent polyester. So, when you talk about purity, you will mean something unadulterated, unmixed.

Again, we can see purity as in the palm wine trade, where you can get the juice a hundred percent, or dilute it with water. Therefore, purity is a heart that does not accept any dilution of truth or contamination with the impurity of thought or impurity born of substandard action. Many years ago, long before I gave my life to Christ, I lived in a place where we would wait by the palm tree for the palm wine tapper to descend. We would then buy the unadulterated palm wine from him. It usually comes in small bottles. In the market, however, the palm wine is sold in gallons. That tells you that what you buy in the market must have undergone 20 - 30 times dilution.

We can understand purity as the opposite of dirt, something unstained, clean, pure, white, dazzling, radiating brilliance, spotlessness, and cleanliness.

Here are other notions of *katharos,* as revealed by Barclay: Barclay says: '*Katharos is regularly used for corn, which has been winnowed or sifted and cleansed of all chaff. It is used of an army which has been purged of all discontented, cowardly, unwilling and inefficient soldiers and composed of first-class fighting men.*'

By way of summary, then, we can say:

'BLESSED ARE THOSE WHOSE MOTIVES ARE PURE AND SINGLE, WHOSE ACTIONS ARE COMPLETELY CLEAN OF DEVIOUS WAYS THAT ARE REMOTE FROM THE TRUTH; AND WHOSE AMBITIONS ARE UNCONTAMINATED BY ALL MANNER OF CARNALITIES.'

When we pause to consider this, we can immediately see why the 'beholding of God' is an extraordinary and uncommon experience. Nevertheless, we must be relentless in our pursuit of purity of heart because we desire to taste that beatific vision where we feel eternity in time.

The Heart of Man

Our next quest is to locate the heart of man – 'Blessed are the pure in heart.' So we need to know exactly what this heart of man represents. Jeremiah, the prophet, stated a revealing truth concerning this quest. *'The human heart is the most deceitful of all things and desperately wicked who really knows how bad it is. But I the Lord, I search all hearts and examine secret motives and give all people their due reward according to what their actions deserve.' (Jeremiah 17:9-10 (NLT2)*

This Scripture sets out the task before us; the heart of the fallen man is deceitful in the core and also desperately wicked. King Solomon had much more to say about the deceitful heart as in Proverbs 26:23-26.

'Smooth lips with an evil heart are like a glaze on an earthen vessel and disguises himself with his speech and harbours deceit within; when he speaks graciously, don't believe him for there are seven detestable things in his heart. Though his hatred is concealed by deception, his evil will be revealed in their assembly.' (CSB Bible)

We may not be as devious as this Scripture describes, but a careful examination of our inward thoughts will reveal that our motives are not always pure and often not consistent with the ideas in our hearts or with actions or words we speak. Only God sees and knows the heart. Little wonder King David reached out to God with a prayer in his heart.

'Search me O God and know my heart test me and know my anxious thoughts, point out anything in me that offends You and lead me in along the path of everlasting life'.
-Psalm 139:33-34 (NLT2)

We need the Holy Spirit's searchlight through God's Word to reveal the depth of impurity that we harbour in our hearts, particularly concerning wicked thoughts and motives. That is why we are told to guard our hearts with diligence in Proverbs 4:23:

Be careful how you think; your life is shaped by your thoughts. (TEV)

This Beatitude is about this constant struggle to keep our thoughts focused on godliness and our motives pure, seeking God's glory in all things. How often do we profess to seek God's glory while the real driving force is gain or personal aggrandizement? It can be tough to keep our focus and motives unadulterated. Man's heart deals with his thoughts, motives, and passions, all of which reside in his soul. All the deception and parading that we do, which do not represent our true intentions, maybe hidden from a fellow-man but are never hidden from God. King David understood this when he stated in Psalm 51:6-7, (NKJV):

'Behold you desire truth in the inward parts, and in the hidden part You will make known to me wisdom. Purge me with hyssop and I shall be clean; wash me, and I shall be whiter than snow.'

Our hearts need to get rid of all our pretensions and godlessness. What helps in this process is the understanding that God knows the actual state of our hearts; He knows our schemes and how we use words to cloak reality when we stretch the truth to a personal advantage and emphasize what requires no emphasis. We see the deception in our motives, and if we can see it, what about the God who sees and knows all things? Apostle John wrote in 1John 3:18-22 (NKJV):

'My little children let us not love in word or tongue, but in deed and in truth and by this we know that we are of the truth and shall assure our hearts before God, for if our hearts condemn us, God is greater than our hearts and knows all things.'

Beloved, if our hearts condemn us not, we have confidence towards God and whatever we ask we receive from Him because we keep His commandments and do those things that are pleasing in His sight.

It is important then to understand why this is so. If we do, we will be able to stop all our gymnastics and cleave to the Lord so our hearts can be rid of all deception. Our Lord Jesus Christ taught that whatever is wrong with us originates in our hearts:

'But those things which proceed out of the mouth come from the heart and they defile a man for out of the heart proceed evil thoughts, murders, adulteries, fornications, theft, false witnesses, blasphemies.'
- Matthew 15:18 (NKJV)

I was on a visit to a city and chanced on a church picnic. On sighting me, the pastor told his people to ask questions that may have bothered them because, according to him, 'I have been a Christian for many years, which is true.' A young man stepped forward, and he asked: "if I have a need in my life and I've sowed a seed repeatedly for that need to be met and nothing has happened so far, should I continue to sow, sow and sow until the need is supplied? Unfortunately, all this young man had understood hitherto, about God, is that the only way to approach Him is to bring Him an offering. If your first offering fails to connect you to His favour, try it again and keep trying until you gain His attention. This approach to God is an example of a truth that has been stretched beyond its context. The Bible teaches that we must not come before God empty-handed in Exodus 23:15 (AMP)

You shall keep the Feast of Unleavened Bread; seven days you shall eat unleavened bread as I commanded you, at the time appointed in the month of Abib, for in it you came out of Egypt. None shall appear before Me empty-handed.

The Bible also says quite categorically in Deuteronomy 10:16 that we cannot bribe God, yet this is the notion that this young man has gained from whomever his teacher was.

'Moses said to Israel, therefore, circumcise the foreskin of your heart and be stiff-necked no longer, for the Lord your God is God of gods and Lord of

lords, the Great God, mighty and awesome who shows no partiality nor takes a bribe.[1]

- Deuteronomy 10:16-17 (NKJV)

Now, we must ask ourselves, how can we purify our hearts? The first thing to note is that our desire to see God must be a driving ambition. It must be at the centre of the drive for intimacy with God. The Bible tells us that our Lord Jesus Christ endured the cross and despised its shame because of the joy that was set before Him. Consequently, He is now seated at the right hand of God. *The hunger to see God and be drawn to Him and into Him must drive this pursuit for inner purity.* Nothing else can do this except a wholesome desire to gain God's best possible on this side of eternity. Once the hunger is there, the Holy Spirit will carefully dissect our motives and guide us to repent and be rid of our hypocrisies, inconsistencies, and pretensions that hinder us.

A preacher once said that God does not always inspire some messages you hear. They are inspired by the Church's statistics, whether the numbers are dwindling or whether there is a need for money. And of course, the preacher comes there and says a lot of things, how God said this and the other, and the God we serve knows that He didn't inspire the message. He knows that the accountant and Church secretary prevailed on the preacher to direct his sermon to address what they consider a vital need in the Church.

When we come through all of that, then we can go before God and say, please, deliver me from such pretensions so that I will bring them a message from heaven every time I come before Your people. When we are driven by this hunger to see God and be one with Him in thought and action, the Holy Spirit will come to our aid. He will assist us to carefully dissect our motives and guide us to repent and be rid of our hypocrisies, inconsistencies as well as all our pretensions. There is nothing as ruinous as self-deception.

God does not change, so He expects us to purify our motives and be consistent with a wholesome pursuit of His honour and glory in our lives. Any notion of self-aggrandizement must be cut off and uprooted before it gains ground and becomes a pattern.

We must also remember that those who sing our praises anywhere can be our worst enemies in a sense. Yes, we cannot control what people say about us, but the day we start to believe them or even worse still start to desire them to say so, then trouble has indeed begun. I recall that the late Gordon Lindsay told a story in one of his books of a notable preacher who was mightily used by God to the extent that the people started to say that he was the Elijah that was to come before Christ's return. The gentleman's position, he said, was that he had no control over what people said about him. Gordon Lindsay said that he and many others around him encouraged the gentleman to denounce it publicly, but he would not, and the whole thing came to an end abruptly as he went home to be with the Lord.

John the Baptist was the Elijah to come before the first advent of our Lord Jesus Christ, but he was content to call himself nothing more than a voice crying out in the wilderness. He taught that he was not worthy to untie the shoes of the Messiah. Our Lord Jesus Christ, later told us that John the Baptist was the Elijah to come. The heart is indeed very deceitful, and before we know it, we are sharing in God's glory and pretending that we are not, yet we are sharing it and enjoying it and expecting it.

We must know that man's spirit is the candle of the LORD, and he hears spoken and unspoken words. He hears every thought; he knows our hearts' real desires as we articulate them in our thoughts, and he watches all that we say both in our hearts and verbally that reflect our true desires. When quickened by the Holy Spirit, he will gently nudge us to get real and consistent. He will teach us how to follow God and to stop using God to satisfy our carnal ambitions. He will teach us like He taught Apostle Paul to say the things that come from God, different from the good ideas he shares as a mature Christian. We see an example of this in 1 Corinthians 7:10 (NKJV):

Now to the married, I command, yet not I but the Lord: A wife is not to depart from her husband.

Again we see a different attestation in another section:

But to the rest I, not the Lord, say: If any brother has a wife who does not believe, and she is willing to live with him, let him not divorce her.
- 1 Corinthians 7:12 (NKJV)

He did not try to use the name of the Lord to gain credibility for what was his personal opinion as a mature Christian. It is so easy for us as leaders to resort to manipulation and control by using the name of the Lord for what was our idea or opinion. The prophet, Jeremiah, had a running battle with false prophets who told their dreams rather than a prophetic word from the Lord. He stated that when we speak for the Lord, it should always be to stir God's people to godly living.

'I have not sent these prophets, yet they ran, I have not spoken to them, yet they prophesied, but if they had stood in My counsel and had caused My people to hear My words, then they would have turned them from their evil way and from the evil of their doings.'
- Jeremiah 23:21-22 (NKJV)

If we receive our messages from the Lord, we will cause God's people to turn from their evil ways and follow their God in holiness and righteousness. When we preach and prophesy, and the people do not move away from their wickedness and corruption, something is fundamentally wrong somewhere. One reason is likely that we did not stand in His counsel to receive the Word that prioritizes the Kingdom of God and His righteousness. We must regularly scrutinize our motives to ensure that they are always as pure as can be. The psalmist said in Psalm 11:7, *'For the Lord is righteous, He loves righteous deeds, the upright shall behold His face,(CSB Bible)*. In other words, 'the upright shall see God.'

The LORD will show us how to walk by faith and trust Him for every blessing, so we never have to organize the 'blessing' on God's behalf. We must always remember that the people who stand before us to hear God's Word will one day stand before the Lord Jesus Christ to give an account of their lives. This is why the Apostle

Paul said to Timothy, in 1 Timothy 4:12-16 (NLT2):

Don't let anyone think less of you because you are young. Be an example to all believers in what you say, in the way you live, in your love, your faith, and your purity.

Until I get there, focus on reading the Scriptures to the Church, encouraging the believers, and teaching them.

Do not neglect the spiritual gift you received through the prophecy spoken over you when the elders of the church laid their hands on you.

Give your complete attention to these matters. Throw yourself into your tasks so that everyone will see your progress.

Keep a close watch on how you live and on your teaching. Stay true to what is right for the sake of your own salvation and the salvation of those who hear you.

That's the tremendous responsibility that we carry so that the Gospel that we preach will save our souls and save the souls of those who listen to us and ensure that if they believe it and follow it, they will get to the shores of eternity with Christ. Now, we must take a bit of time to look at the God we serve. The Bible tells us He is absolute purity. Therefore, when our Lord Jesus tells us that 'Blessed are the pure in heart,' He is talking about what Amos was saying in Amos 3:3 *'Two must agree before they can walk together.'* So when you and I pursue inner purity, we draw close to God because He is absolute purity.

'This is the message we have heard from our Lord Jesus Christ and declare to you that God is light and in Him is no darkness at all if we say we have fellowship with God and walk in darkness we lie and do not practice the truth.'
-1John 1:5-6 (NKJV)

Only by the Holy Spirit through the Word can we have our spirits purged of all that offends. Now, remember that if we come to God through Christ, He invests us with the righteousness of Christ. He admonishes us to walk in holiness before Him because He is holy as revealed in 1 Peter 1:13-16 (NLT2):

So think clearly and exercise self-control. Look forward to the gracious salvation that will come to you when Jesus Christ is revealed to the world.

So you must live as God's obedient children. Don't slip back into your old ways of living to satisfy your own desires. You didn't know any better then.

But now you must be holy in everything you do, just as God who chose you is holy.

For the Scriptures say, "You must be holy because I am holy."

Our pursuit of holiness and inner purity must be sincere and total. We know and have been told in Hebrews 12:12-14 (TEV):

167

Lift up your tired hands, then, and strengthen your trembling knees!

Keep walking on straight paths, so that the lame foot may not be disabled, but instead be healed.

Try to be at peace with everyone, and try to live a holy life, because no one will see the Lord without it.

The path to holy living is uncomplicated. We need to ask the Holy Spirit to search our hearts, direct our thoughts, and guide our footsteps. I always try to ask Him to search my heart and fathom my deepest motives so that I will not indulge in self-deception. We must never forget that if our stated and unstated purposes are not pure, many of those who follow us will know it but may not say anything to us.

We must not hesitate to self-correct when the Holy Spirit demands it, at the very least privately making the necessary changes. This is one of the most challenging but essential things to do for those who pursue inner purity before the Lord.

Our repentance must always be genuine so that it can result in change. The proof of repentance is the change as John the Baptist preached in Matthew 3:8 *'Bring forth fruits worthy of repentance.'* When we lead godly lives, the LORD will be delighted to bless us so that our lives will reveal the wonders of His grace.

Iniquity is atoned for by loyalty and faithfulness, and one turns from evil by the fear of the Lord.
When a person's ways please the Lord, he makes even his enemies to be at peace with him.
Better a little with righteousness than great income with injustice.
- Proverbs 16:6-8 (CSB Bible)

'Blessed are the pure in heart for they shall see God.' This is the mother and father of all overhauls. To go from indulgent sinners to seeking purity of our actions and then graduate to the purity of our thoughts and passions is a very significant

change in our lives that will lead to a tangible transformation in our character.

The pure in heart will have the opportunity and privilege of a deeper fellowship with God. The Lord will abide with them and reveal Himself to them and cause their souls to drink from the depth of His wisdom and knowledge. They will constantly receive the communion of the Holy Spirit. The Counsellor will instruct them daily to walk in God's will so that they may be blessed. We must always remember that carnality diminishes inner purity. The reward for the pursuit of holiness and inner purity is seen clearly in Psalm 112:1-10 (NKJV):

Praise the LORD! Blessed is the man who fears the LORD, Who delights greatly in His commandments.
His descendants will be mighty on earth; The generation of the upright will be blessed.
Wealth and riches will be in his house, And his righteousness endures forever.

Unto the upright there arises light in the darkness; He is gracious, and full of compassion, and righteous.

A good man deals graciously and lends; He will guide his affairs with discretion.

Surely he will never be shaken; The righteous will be in everlasting remembrance.

He will not be afraid of evil tidings; His heart is steadfast, trusting in the LORD.

His heart is established; He will not be afraid, Until he sees his desire upon his enemies.

He has dispersed abroad, He has given to the poor; His righteousness endures forever; His horn will be exalted with honour.

The wicked will see it and be grieved; He will gnash his teeth and melt away; The desire of the wicked shall perish.

Blessed are the pure in heart for they shall see God.' God will be their companion. Through His Holy Spirit, God's presence will overshadow them, and the wisdom of God will be with them.

PRAYER

Lord, please forgive my hypocrisies; forgive my pretensions at godliness. Please show me Your ways, and teach me Your paths. I desire to live daily in Your presence and commune with You, my God. I desire to see Your glory and experience Your incredible power and majesty; to fellowship daily in Your presence and commune with Your Spirit. Father, this is my heart's desire, and Lord may Your Spirit come mightily upon my soul and take away the garbage, take away the filth and give me inner purity in Jesus' name. Amen.

CHAPTER 7

BLESSED ARE THE PEACEMAKERS

'Blessed are the peacemakers, for they shall
be called sons of God.'
- Matthew 5:9

We come to the challenge of peacemaking. Peacemakers make peace, but 'what is peace?' We must be sure of what we mean so that we might enter into the business of making peace and being instruments of peace. When He sent forth His disciples to preach, our Lord Jesus Christ included peace in His instructions in Luke 10:5, He said, *"Whatever house you enter, first say, 'Peace to the Household.'* *If a person of peace is there,*

your peace will rest on him, but if not, it will return to you." (NKJV)

In the Middle East, *Shalom* or *Salam* is a standard Hebrew greeting. To the Hebrew, this peace is not just the absence of trouble but includes everything that makes for a person's well-being and highest good. So when you say, *Shalom* or *Peace*, you wish them not just the absence of trouble, but you are praying for everything that makes for their well-being, their comfort, or their highest good.

In the same way, *Salam*, which means the same thing as *Shalom*, is both the absence of evil and the presence of everything good. This is the way Barclays' Bible describes it. "What this means in effect is that the blessing of this Beatitude is to do everything you can to ensure good." We also know that the blessing is on the peacemaker, who, whenever found in a situation with great potential for trouble, enters with wisdom and courage to tease it apart and find where the truth lies so that peace that evolves will be according to the truth. This is not the peacemaking that avoids issues and sweeps them under the carpet, but find the peace that confronts the problems and may displease people when they come face to face with the truth in their situation. This peace is not possible without forgiveness, honesty, and love. It is, therefore, the peace that is inspired by the life of our Lord Jesus Christ, who came down to solve the problems of man's iniquity before God Almighty by personal sacrifice.

WE MUST BE CAREFUL THEN TO AVOID THAT KIND OF PEACE THAT EVADES ISSUES, OR THAT YIELDS TO INJUSTICE AND OPPRESSION FOR THE SAKE OF PEACE. THIS IS THE KIND OF PEACE THAT ONLY POSTPONES THE EVIL DAY, FOR

PEACEMAKING MUST ALWAYS APPROACH CONFLICT RESOLUTION BY GETTING THE PARTIES TO HAVE THE COURAGE TO CONFRONT THE TRUTH OF THEIR ERRORS, WEAKNESSES, AND FAILINGS.

In making peace with man through judicial pardon, the Lord God Almighty predestines that those so pardoned must rise to lead a new life after the model of Christ as revealed in Romans 6:4-7:

Therefore we were buried with Him through baptism into death, that just as Christ was raised out of death by the glory of the Father, even so we also should walk in newness of life. For if we have been united together in the likeness of His death, certainly, we also shall be in the likeness of His resurrection, knowing this, that our old man was crucified with Him, that the body of sin might be done away with, that we should no longer be slaves to sin. For He who has died has been freed from sin. (NKJV)

This is the peace that carries responsibility because it always comes with the price of forgiveness, self-sacrificing love, and self-denial. It is a studied peace rather than an emotional peace with little or no content because it has failed to address the issues in the discord. In conclusion, this Beatitude demands not the passive acceptance of things because we are afraid of the trouble of doing anything about them, but the active phrasing of the issues while acknowledging that the way to peace may still be a struggle.

Now, let us go to the peace of the peacemakers. Making this peace is something that the Lord God Almighty did in Christ Jesus. The apostle Paul put it this way in Romans 5:1-2.

'Therefore, having been justified by faith, we have peace with God through our Lord Jesus Christ, through whom also we have access by faith into this grace in which we stand, and rejoice in the hope of the glory of God.' (NKJV)

This is why peacemakers are called sons of God or people who act like God. We can look at peacemaking in three dimensions:

The first are those who lead others to make peace with God through our Lord and Saviour Jesus Christ.

Quite a few would say this is not what our Lord Jesus had in mind. But this is essential peacemaking that has the potential to turn a trouble maker into a peacemaker. Peace with God always begins the journey into transforming an individual into the nature and character of Christ. As he conforms into the image of Christ, he develops into a peacemaker that can reconcile men one to another. When we show others how to make peace with our God through the forgiveness of sin and acceptance of Jesus Christ as the Lord of their lives, we can steer them to a life of peace with God that gives rise to other dimensions of peace in our lives and our world.

Quite a few are lost to the truth that man cannot save himself and that God is angry with the wicked every day. The wrath of God is always channelled to the children of disobedience who live lives of perpetual sinfulness. When we lead men to have peace with God, we take them to a new and a higher pedestal from which they can look at life more comprehensively.

The next peace is inner peace. We are often in a struggle for one thing or another, and as a result, we lose our peace or inner quiet. Saint Augustine had this to say about this struggle for inner peace, *'There is in the inner person a kind of daily quarrel, a praiseworthy battle to keep what is better* *from being overcome by what is worse. The struggle is to keep the desire from dominating the mind. We also must keep lust from conquering wisdom."*

This is the stable peace that you and I ought to develop in ourselves so that the better in us may be in charge of what is worse. The better in us is the part in which God's image is found. This is called the mind, the intellect, or, more generically, the soul. There, faith burns, hope receives strength, and the fire of love comes alive. You will learn the peace that comes through the pursuit of God's will. When we are in His will and face challenges, faith comes without a struggle because we were led into the situation and have high expectations of God that He will rise to meet every need to His glory and for the fulfilment of His purposes through us. This is the source of this inner peace.

Therefore, when we follow God, working in His will, and encounter challenges, we are not shaken or troubled because we have faith that the God who led us into the place where we encountered problems He will make provision. This is the awesome reality displayed by Elijah, the prophet, when he said to King Ahab in 1 Kings 17:1, *"Until I say so, there will be no rain here."* God Himself spoke to Elijah, *"Go to the Brook Cherith, I have made provision for you. The ravens will bring you food morning and evening."*

Now when the brook dried up, God again said, *"Go to Zarephath. There, I have made another provision."* So, these experiences that men like Elijah had with God that come from obedience to God in the Bible teach us that inner peace comes when we align with God's will, particularly when following God's way. It does not preclude challenges and problems, but it gives faith that God will see us through the situation we find ourselves.

The third one is peace between men.

Two variants of this exist; one is seeking peace with my neighbour, and the other is being a mediator of peace between man and his fellow man.

1. Taking responsibility for living in peace with my neighbour

The Bible calls this the pursuit of peace, which is part of a Christian's life walking daily in the fear of God. King David affirms this in Psalm 34:11-14 (NRSV):

Come, O children, listen to me; I will teach you the fear of the LORD.

Which of you desires life, and covets many days to enjoy good?

Keep your tongue from evil, and your lips from speaking deceit.

Depart from evil, and do good; seek peace, and pursue it.

This is the lifestyle of the man or woman who fears the Lord. They must be daily engaged in the pursuit of peace with their fellow men or women. A husband with his wife walking daily in love must also walk daily in peace and harmony. Here the psalmist says that this is how to prolong our lives on the earth and enjoy a good life. This also shows that the fear of God is ruling our hearts, and so controls our actions. When we depart from evil and deceit and show that we fear the Lord by pursuing peace, we prolong our days on the earth. As a general principle, the Bible admonishes us in Romans 14:19, '*Therefore, let us pursue the things which make for peace and the things by which we may edify one another.*' *(NKJV)*

We learn from this that peace is a choice we make daily in our relationships through forbearance.

Timothy was a youthful Christian leader brought up by the Apostle Paul. Here we see the counsel the Apostle Paul gave him in 2 Timothy 2:22-26:

"Flee also youthful lusts; but pursue righteousness, faith, love and peace with those who call on the Lord out of a pure heart But avoid foolish and ignorant disputes knowing that they generate strife. And the servant of the Lord must not quarrel but be gentle to all, able to teach, patient; in humility correcting those who are in opposition, if God perhaps will grant them repentance so that they may know the truth so that they can come to their senses and escape the sneer of the devil, having been taken captive by him to do his will." (NKJV)

In my personal life, I was moved deeply by verse 24: "And the servant of the LORD must not quarrel or strive:" I repeatedly used it to counsel myself and others. The simple way of understanding this is that as Christians, we must not strive or fight but must pursue peace in all our relationships by avoiding unnecessary arguments and disputes. Also, we need humility to be able to continue this peace in our relationships.

This humility requires us to bend over and hear the other person out and be convinced of their viewpoint's merit or demerit. Those who merely state their views without listening to the other person suffer myopia that will not allow peace to thrive. Humility allows us to concede when we are wrong and state our perspective without aggression or a dictatorial finality; it is my way, or there will be no way.

The other virtue most needed in a peacemaker is patience. It is not always that we see a particular point of view that will make for peace immediately we are confronted with it. So, as peacemakers, we must be patient in our relationships to state and restate a truth in love until the Holy Spirit enlarges the neighbour's understanding to embrace the truth. In Hebrews 12:14, we learn that the pursuit of peace and holiness must go together if we ever hope to see the Lord God Almighty and walk daily with Him, in this world, and eternity.

To be God's peacemakers and so children of God, which means children who act like God our Father in heaven, each of us has a personal responsibility to strive for peace in our relationships.

Here is Apostle Peter admonishing in
1 Peter 3:8-12:

"Finally, everyone must live in harmony, be sympathetic, love one another, have compassion, and be humble. Don't pay people back evil for the evil they do to you or ridicule those who ridicule you. Instead, bless them because you are called to inherit a blessing. People who are called to live a full life and enjoy good days must keep their tongues from saying evil things and their lips from speaking deceitful things. They

must turn away from evil and do good; they must seek peace and pursue it. The Lord's eyes are on those who do what He approves; His ears hear their prayers. The Lord confronts those who do evil." (GW)

We are to live in harmony. Harmony is a word best understood in music. We are to be different instruments in an orchestral blend.

When we take personal responsibility to live in peace, we produce relationships that are in tune, in harmony with godly living principles. This will introduce joy in our relationships. And part of that harmony is not to repay evil with evil. It is also to control what we say to another person. Those who pursue peace are not in the habit of using hurtful words. The Apostle Peter says, *"..and with that, you will not be out to increase strife and discord but to make peace."* Act in love, and this is agape or unconditional love, which makes peace easier. Have compassion. When your actions create unhappiness and misery, put yourself in the other's shoes and recoil so you can give peace a chance.

2. Being a mediator of peace among men: It is always a great responsibility for the peacemaker to have the opportunity to mediate peace between two warring or opposing factions. Here are the things you must note.

i. The first thing to note is if we are to make peace without truth, such peace will not last unless in a slave-master relationship. Peace in a slave-master relationship is an imposed peace and not a just or fair peace. To produce a just peace, we must act according to the truth; but can one always determine truth? This is where mediation must reach out to godliness so that the more spiritually mature can concede their rights for peace to reign.

Peace can be challenging and complicated with the spiritually immature yet to imbibe Christ-like character of self-denial and self-sacrifice. The truth in this Beatitude is to inspire us to be like God in peacemaking, forgiving the wrong, and refusing to pay evil with evil for peace. Peacemaking is to find the truth, condemn the wrong, and urge forgiveness and love to enable us to be children of God.

Now, here is Barclays again on peacemaking by mediation. "*There are people who are always storm-centers of trouble and bitterness and strife wherever they are. They are either involved in quarrels themselves or the cause of quarrel between others. They are trouble makers. There are people like that in almost every society and every Church. And such people are doing the devil's work.*

On the other hand, thank God that there are people in whose presence bitterness can not live. People who bridge the gulf and heal the breaches, sweeten the bitterness; such people are doing the God-like work. For it is the great purpose of God to bring peace between man and Himself, and between man and his fellow man. The man who divides men is doing the devil's work, but the man who unites men is doing God's work."

In conclusion, to appreciate this Beatitude, *'Blessed are the peacemakers for they are children of God,'* those who act like God our Father in this world have found peace with God and lead and help others find peace with God.

ii. Secondly, through the manifestations of the fruit of the Holy Spirit, they have found peace in themselves and are working daily to find and maintain peace with others.

iii. Thirdly, they have become vessels in the Holy Spirit's hands to help others find peace between man and his fellow men.

There are a few pertinent questions as we bring this to an end:

1. Are you and I peacemakers?

2. Have you found peace with God for yourself?

3. Are you walking daily to pursue peace with others, with everyone around you?

4. Have you grown to become a vessel in God's hand used to make peace between a man and his fellow man - whether they be husband and wife, siblings, colleagues, and others?

God is calling us to embrace peace with God first and then to embrace peace in our hearts and peace with our neighbours; and offer ourselves willingly to God, no matter the sacrifice, to be agents of peace between man and his fellow man.

PRAYER

Father, make me an instrument of Your peace so that wherever there is discord, I will bring unity and love. Give me wisdom, give me understanding, show me how to walk in harmony with all the people around me so that I will be a child of God indeed, for You said, *"Blessed are the peacemakers; they do the work of God on earth."* Holy Spirit, breathe Your life upon us, that we may become peacemakers everywhere we go.

Lord, I pray for every family where there is discord, may Your peace rest upon them that they will rise and make peace according to truth and godliness, that the order they find will last. I thank You, O God, for, in Jesus' mighty name, I pray. Amen

CHAPTER 8

BLESSED ARE THOSE PERSECUTED FOR RIGHTEOUSNESS SAKE

'Blessed are those who are persecuted for righteousness sake, for theirs is the kingdom of heaven. Blessed are you when they revile and persecute you, and say all kinds of evil against you falsely for My sake. Rejoice and be exceedingly glad for great is your reward in heaven, for so they persecuted the prophets who were before you.'
- Matthew 5:10 -12

I would like to join those who say that there are eight beatitudes instead of nine. When you look at it closely, you will see that verses ten to twelve speak of various persecutions. Whereas verse ten speaks of physical abuse of the sort being suffered by Christians in Northern Nigeria and many other parts of the world today; verses eleven to twelve speak of verbal persecution that is global and occurs in practically every nation of the world.

'Blessed are those who are persecuted for righteousness sake for theirs is the kingdom of heaven.' Now, what exactly is persecution for righteousness sake? O how happy are those who face persecution for righteousness sake, for to them belongs God's Kingdom. Observe that two Beatitudes carry this reward, "for theirs is the kingdom of God."

The first beatitude says, *'Blessed are the poor in spirit for theirs is the kingdom of heaven;'* then, the eighth beatitude says, *'Blessed are those persecuted for righteousness sake, for theirs is the kingdom of heaven.'* So now, what do these two have in common? When we have poverty of the spirit, it is proof that we understand our status outside of God's grace; God's mercy is our only hope of entering into God's kingdom. Having entered the kingdom of God on earth, we begin to walk in righteousness before God. This draws the ungodly and the unbeliever's wrath, particularly those who stand to lose by our pursuit of godliness. But notice that it is the fact that we face persecution for righteousness sake that proves that our repentance and conversion is genuine.

We have supporting Scriptures that tell us that salvation without righteousness is a farce. First is the Sermon on the Mount where our Lord and Saviour Jesus Christ said in Matthew 6:33, *'But seek ye first the kingdom of God and His righteousness and all these things shall be added to you.'* Again, He said to his disciples in Matthew 5:20, *'But I say to you that unless your righteousness exceeds the righteousness of the Scribes and Pharisees, you will by no means enter the kingdom of heaven.'*

Our Lord Jesus Christ expects a higher degree of the practice of righteousness from those who seek to enter the Kingdom of God by becoming His disciples. They spend their days on earth working out or practicalizing their salvation in fear and trembling. There is a sense in which persecution for righteousness or godliness is an authenticating experience that shows that our salvation is genuine, as revealed in 2 Timothy 3:12 *'Yes! And all who desire to live godly in Christ Jesus will suffer persecution.'*

We never go out into the world as Christians to provoke persecution. However, the moment we stand with God on the earth and stand against evil, immorality, sexual perversions, and bribery and corruption, we will inevitably draw persecutions with strings because of the opposition by those who stand to gain by the rot that currently prevails. The Bible has a clear example in Acts 19:24-41, where Demetrius gathered the silversmith and the goldsmith union to cause a riot because of Paul's teachings that any god made with human hands is not and cannot be the true God.

Now, should the opposition stop such a message of light that drives away darkness from being preached? The answer is no, a thousand times. Any god made with human hands cannot be the true God, and I dare to add that any God that you can carry in your pocket or your bag or even in your car cannot be the true God. The Apostle Paul encouraged Timothy, his protégé, to keep growing in God's power despite any opposition in 2 Timothy 3:10-17 (ISV):

But you have observed my teaching, my way of life, my purpose, my faith, my patience, my love, my endurance, and my persecutions and sufferings that happened to me in Antioch, Iconium, and Lystra.

What persecutions I endured! Yet the Lord rescued me from all of them.

Indeed, all who want to live a godly life in union with Christ Jesus will be persecuted.

But evil people and impostors will go from bad to worse as they deceive others and are themselves deceived.

But as for you, continue in what you have learned and found to be true because you know from whom you learned it.

From infancy, you have known the Holy Scriptures that can give you the wisdom you need for salvation through faith in Christ Jesus.

All Scripture is inspired by God and is useful for teaching, for reproof, for correction, and for training in righteousness, so that the man of God may be complete and thoroughly equipped for every good work.

But we must not miss the significance of his confessed victory over all his troubles. He stated that he had to endure some persecutions while they lasted, but in the end, the Lord delivered him out of them all. As a result of these experiences, he could write to the Ephesian Christians in Ephesians 6:10-12, *"Finally my brethren be strong in the Lord and in the power of His might. Put on the whole armour of God, that you may be able to stand against the wiles of the devil, for we do not wrestle against flesh and blood, but against principalities, against powers, against the rulers of the darkness of this age, against spiritual wickedness, in the heavenly places."*

Now we begin to appreciate what our Lord Jesus had in mind when He said, *"Blessed are those who are persecuted for righteousness."* These are the men and women who decide to stand daily on the truth of God's Word: they will take their bearing and moral values from God's Word. They will insist that we must live life according to God's Word and the revelation that came to us through our Lord Jesus Christ. They are men and women who are ready not to compromise the truth for whatever reason and, as a result of that insistence on God's Word, draw enemies with strings, all manners of enemies for whatever reasons. The Apostle Paul said, *'I went through it: I suffered it at Lystra. I suffered it at Iconium. I suffered it at Antioch, but through them all, the Lord delivered me.'*

Since persecution is inevitable, the way the Bible states it, we have to learn how to contend with opposition and come out victorious, as the Apostle Paul said. Here in Ephesians 6:10-11, he told us that the secret is to be strong in the Lord and to be strong in the power of God's might. We must ponder this text of Scripture and pause to ask ourselves: 'How can a Christian be strong in the Lord and in the power of His might?

The first thing we must notice is that we must never give room to the devil, as the Apostle admonished the Ephesians in chapter 4, verse 27.

But to put his advice in context, let us read his entire admonition from Ephesians 4:22-32 (TEV):

22 So get rid of your old self, which made you live as you used to – the old self that was being destroyed by its deceitful desires.

23 Your hearts and minds must be made completely new,

24 and you must put on the new self, which is created in God's likeness and reveals itself in the true life that is upright and holy.

25 No more lying, then! Each of you must tell the truth to the other believer because we are all members together in the body of Christ.

26 If you become angry, do not let your anger lead you into sin, and do not stay angry all day.

27 Don't give the Devil a chance.

28 If you used to rob, you must stop robbing and start working, in order to earn an honest living for yourself and to be able to help the poor.

29 Do not use harmful words, but only helpful words, the kind that build up and provide what is needed, so that what you say will do good to those who hear you.

30 And do not make God's Holy Spirit sad; for the Spirit is God's mark of ownership on you, a guarantee that the Day will come when God will set you free.

31 Get rid of all bitterness, passion, and anger: no more shouting or insults, no more hateful feelings of any sort.

32 Instead, be kind and tender-hearted to one another, and forgive one another, as God has forgiven you through Christ.

Now, how does sin hinder our empowerment in the struggle against the forces of darkness? In the Book of Ephesians, we see that even though the human agent will organize and execute persecution against believers, there are spiritual forces behind it. And this is why we need to be strong in the Lord when we pass through persecutions. We need the inner strength and courage the Holy Spirit provides to stand firm despite every pressure. We learn a little more about this in Zechariah 3:1-10 (TEV):

1 In another vision, the LORD showed me the High Priest Joshua standing before the Angel of the LORD. And there beside Joshua stood Satan, ready to bring an accusation against him.

2 The Angel of the LORD said to Satan, "May the LORD condemn you, Satan! May the LORD, who loves Jerusalem, condemn you. This man is like a stick snatched from the fire."

3 Joshua was standing there, wearing filthy clothes.

4 The Angel said to his heavenly attendants, "Take away the filthy clothes this man is wearing." Then, he said to Joshua, "I have taken away your sin and will give you new clothes to wear."

5 He commanded the attendants to put a clean turban on Joshua's head. They did so, and then they put the new clothes on him while the Angel of the LORD stood there.

6 Then the Angel told Joshua that

7 the LORD Almighty had said: "If you obey my laws and perform the duties I have assigned you, then you will continue to be in charge of my Temple and its courts, and I will hear your prayers, just as I hear the prayers of the angels who are in my presence.

8 Listen then, Joshua, you who are the High Priest; and listen, you fellow priests of his, you that are the sign of a good future: I will reveal my servant, who is called The Branch!

9 I am placing in front of Joshua a single stone with seven facets. I will engrave an inscription on it, and in a single day I will take away the sin of this land.

10 When that day comes, each of you will invite your neighbour to come and enjoy peace and security, surrounded by your vineyards and fig trees."

There is an accuser of believers who is continually bringing our failures before God. To empower Joshua, the Lord God Almighty had to purge his sins and change his status. This is similar to what He did for Isaiah in Isaiah 6:5-8 (TEV):

5 I said, "There is no hope for me! I am doomed because every word that passes my lips is sinful, and I live among a people whose every word is sinful. And yet, with my own eyes, I have seen the King, the LORD Almighty."

6 Then one of the creatures flew down to me, carrying a burning coal that he had taken from the altar with a pair of tongs.

7 He touched my lips with the burning coal and said: "This has touched your lips, and now, your guilt is gone, and your sins are forgiven."

8 Then I heard the Lord say, "Whom shall I send? Who will be our messenger?" I answered, "I will go! Send me!"

WE MUST NOTE THAT SIN IS THE MAJOR OBSTACLE TO EMPOWERMENT AND COMMISSIONING.

Isaiah needed to be cleaned up; Joshua, the high priest, also had to be cleaned up. In Joshua's case, the Angel admonished him to stay clean so that God could empower him by answering his prayers. Did you notice that the cleaned-up Joshua and his fellow priests are called the signs of a good future in Zechariah 3:8? When they begin to minister righteousness to God's people, their nation's sins will be wiped away in one day.

Let us take a much closer look at Zacharias 3:8-10 (TEV):

"Listen then Joshua, you who are the high priest and listen you fellow priests of his, you that are a sign of a good future; I will reveal My servant who is called the BRANCH. I am placing in front of Joshua, a single stone with seven facets. I will engrave an inscription on it, and in a single day, I will take away the sin of this land. When that day comes, each of you will invite your neighbours to come and enjoy the peace

and security surrounded by your vineyard and fig trees."

The Branch is our Lord and Saviour Jesus Christ. He came to wipe away our sins and to empower His saints as revealed in Revelations 12:10-12 (TEV):

10 Then I heard a loud voice in heaven saying, "Now God's salvation has come! Now God has shown His power as King! Now His Messiah has shown His authority! For the one who stood before our God and accused believers day and night has been thrown out of heaven.

11 They won the victory over him by the blood of the Lamb and by the truth which they proclaimed, and they were willing to give up their lives and die.

12 And so be glad, you heavens, and all you that live there! But how terrible for the earth and the sea! For the devil has come down to you, and he is filled with rage because he knows that he has only a little time left."

Now the saints overcome the devil by the blood of Jesus. How? Because they use the blood of Jesus to wipe away their sins, thereby rendering the accusations of the devil ineffective. Each time we fail God and come before Him penitent, wiping away our sins with the blood of Jesus, we render the devil's accusations powerless. Also, when we do that, we receive power from God to testify to the truth as it is in Jesus Christ even at the risk of our lives. There is another dimension to this victory, which God designed to empower His people. The revelation is in verse 12, *'And so be glad you Heavens and all you that live there.'* You may wonder, 'Do you and I live in heaven?' Read Philippians 3:17-21

"Keep on imitating me, my friends. Pay attention to those who follow the right examples that we have set for you. I've told you this many times before, and now I repeat it with tears. There are many whose lives make them enemies of Christ's death on the cross.

They are going to end up in hell because their god is their bodily desires, they are proud of what they should be ashamed of, and they think only of things that belong to this world. However, we are citizens of heaven and we eagerly wait for our Saviour the Lord Jesus Christ to come from heaven. He will change our weak mortal bodies and make them like His own glorious body, using that power by which He is able to bring all things under His glory."

Here is the revelation - Although we live on earth, when we come to Christ, the Bible says we become citizens of heaven. So, we are citizens of heaven passing through this earth. This is similar to the impact of dual citizenship, a common scenario during the COVID-19 or Corona pandemic; Say your sibling has a British or American passport. He gets a call that USA or UK is coming to evacuate her citizens. And one day, the plane arrives, and off he goes. Though he was living here in Nigeria, he's a citizen of the USA or the UK, so they came for him.

CHRISTIANS ARE CALLED TO BE CITIZENS OF HEAVEN PASSING THROUGH THE EARTH, RATHER THAN CITIZENS OF EARTH TRYING TO GET TO HEAVEN.

As citizens of heaven on earth, the devil, displaced from heaven to earth does not control us, because we have the wherewithal to nullify his greatest weapon against us, which is sin. The potent weapon is the Blood of Jesus, which washes away the sins of all those who come to Him by faith. When we repent of our sins and symbolically wash them in the Blood of Jesus by faith, the devil's power to accuse us before God is rendered impotent. The Blood of Jesus enables us to maintain our residency in heaven while passing through the earth.

And besides, citizens of heaven passing through the earth may face diverse persecutions, but because their citizenship of heaven empowers them, help is always available. This was the point that the Angel made to Joshua, the high priest," *If you obey My commandments and walk in righteousness, I will answer your prayers and give you victory over the devil. I will answer your prayers, and you will have free and privileged access to come in and out of My presence.*"

This is the tremendous privilege of walking in righteousness before the Lord. As believers, we must covet this because that's how we can be empowered to drive darkness out of our lives. When we stand in truth and righteousness before God, heaven will release manifold blessings into our lives. Also, the power of the Holy Spirit will manifest in and through our lives.

Now the Bible says, '*Blessed are those who are persecuted for righteousness sake:* Although we face persecutions for righteousness sake, the Bible is not saying that we should be sitting ducks waiting for the enemy to come and mow us down. The Apostle said to Timothy, "*I was persecuted, and I had to endure quite a bit of it, but God delivered me from all of it in the end.*" Therefore, we must understand the secret to divine empowerment, which enables us to defeat the enemy while passing through the world as citizens of heaven. We are to be strong in the Lord and in the power of His might, and there is no way to be empowered except through righteousness and prayer.

14 For this reason, I fall on my knees before the Father,

15 from whom every family in heaven and on earth receives its true name.

16 I ask God from the wealth of his glory to give you power through His Spirit to be strong in your inner selves,

17 and I pray that Christ will make his home in your hearts through faith. I pray that you may have your roots and foundation in love,

18 so that you, together with all God's people, may have the power to understand how broad and long, how high and deep, is Christ's love.

19 Yes, may you come to know his love – although it can never be fully known – and so be completely filled with the very nature of God.

- Ephesians 3:14-19 (TEV)

Verse 19 shows that if I understand how to walk in love and continue to walk in love, the revelation of God's nature and the impartation of God's nature will come to me, and the Lord and I will be in synchrony in my life. And that's how power transfer occurs to endorse my spiritual authority in the world. With this authority, I alter the balance of power in conflicts in and around my life and world. The LORD God Almighty wants you and I to be empowered for inner strength. We see this in the lyrics of the song that says: *"even in winter, it is summer in my life."* We must know that God has given us the authority to stop principalities and powers that orchestrate all these persecutions. Here is the Scriptural authority: Ephesians 3:20,

'To Him who is working in us is able to do so much more than we can ever ask for or even think of, to God be the glory. The glory is in the Church and the Church, the body of Christ is you and I who believe. To Him be Glory in the Church Christ Jesus for all time forever and ever. Amen'

For instance, there is an infusion of spiritual energy into our human spirit that gives us the inner strength, the boldness, and the courage to walk in love and destroy the root cause of corruption: selfishness and greed. Genuine compassion for the oppressed, the poor, and the marginalized causes us to stamp out corruption and use the resources available to us to care for the people, no matter where we find ourselves. And once we begin to enter into the fuller dimensions of the revelation of love, all corruption and evil vanish because we realize that we should treat our neighbours the way we expect them to treat us as Jesus our Lord taught us. That will set opposition against us for sure, but the Holy Spirit's empowerment fills us with God's fullness; the inner resources made available to us from heaven empowers us to hold steady under pressure until victory comes.

Help comes to us from heaven orchestrated by our Father in heaven. A Christian is not supposed to go out there and wait for the world and the devil to smother him, absolutely not. Through prayer and the exercise of spiritual authority, we are to pre-empt the opposition forces and thwart their plans against us.

19 Listen! I have given you authority, so that you can walk on snakes and scorpions and overcome all the power of the Enemy, and nothing will hurt you. 20 But don't be glad because the evil spirits obey you; rather be glad because your names are written in heaven."

- Luke 10:19-20 (TEV)

Permissions and Authorisations

The Scriptures reveal that whatever we see in the natural must have its origin in the spiritual. We learn from the Book of Job that there was a day in heaven when particular permission was granted to the devil concerning Job's life, and then, there was a day on earth when the devil executed that permission. What empowers the devil to seek permission is a list of accusations that he tables before Almighty God against the

THE BEATITUDES

individual. He is called the accuser of the brethren in Revelations 12:10.

10Then I heard a triumphant voice in heaven proclaiming:

"Now salvation and power are set in place, and the kingdom reign of our God and the ruling authority of his Anointed One are established.

For the accuser of our brothers and sisters, who relentlessly accused them day and night before our God, has now been defeated – cast out once and for all!
- Revelation 12:10 (Passion NTPsa)

To counter these charges by the devil and deny him permission before God, the Christian must repent of all known sins and wash clean by faith in the Blood of Jesus. The Scriptures declare that the saints overcame the devil by the Blood of the Lamb - the Blood of Jesus.

11 They conquered him completely through the blood of the Lamb and the powerful word of his testimony.

217

They triumphed because they did not love and cling to their own lives, even when faced with death.

- Revelation 12:11 (Passion NTPsa)

As believers who understand spiritual warfare, we know the power of true repentance for blocking the devil and his plans. Persistence in sin or refusal to repent all aid the enemy, but when we repent, there is restoration. Then we can go to the Father for empowerment, for refilling, for renewal.

We need to understand the connection between sin, repentance, and empowerment. Anyone who seriously wants to be empowered must maintain the relationship we have with God Almighty through His Son Jesus Christ. Quite a few people cannot see this connection, and still, they wonder why they are not effective in their exercise of spiritual authority. As we saw earlier, Joshua, the high priest, came before God to be empowered in Zachariah chapter 3, but the devil was there to accuse him. The wonderful thing that happened there was that God rejected the devil's accusation, and by the act of sovereign grace, forgave Joshua his sins and empowered him.

Power and righteousness go together because the Bible says that God's throne is established in righteousness. What does it mean by that? If God were not completely righteous, He would not exercise power and authority over all creation. Because no creature can match His purity, righteousness, or holiness, no creature can match His power.

The System of Empowerment for Man

To make it easier for man to be empowered before God, He sent His Son Jesus Christ to establish the forgiveness of sins for humanity so that we can appear before God as holy as Christ.

21 At one time you were far away from God and were his enemies because of the evil things you did and thought.

22 But now, by means of the physical death of his Son, God has made you his friends, in order to bring you, holy, pure, and faultless, into his presence.

- Colossians 1:21-22 (TEV)

We are to use the Blood of Jesus to position ourselves properly before God as faultless and blameless.

7 But if we walk in the light as He is in the light, we have fellowship with one another, and the blood of Jesus Christ His Son cleanses us from all sin.

- 1 John 1:7 (NKJV)

This provision stands, and we are encouraged to stay clean every day. But if perchance we slip up, we must return to renew our peace with God through Jesus Christ His Son.

1 I am writing this to you, my children, so that you will not sin, but if anyone does sin, we have someone who pleads with the Father on our behalf—Jesus Christ, the righteous one.

2 And Christ himself is the means by which our sins are forgiven, and not our sins only, but also the sins of everyone.

- 1 John 2:1-2 (TEV)

This is the way our Lord Jesus Christ walked this earth - without sin. He was controlled from heaven, and He did God's will on earth as it is done in heaven. As a result, He had a continuous flow of God's power to endorse and enforce His authority on earth.

34 The one whom God has sent speaks God's words, because God gives him the fullness of his Spirit.

35 The Father loves his Son and has put everything in his power.

Our Lord Jesus Christ revealed to us the secret to His power and authority while He was here on earth:

- John 3:34-35 (TEV)

27 They did not understand that Jesus was talking to them about the Father.

28 So he said to them, "When you lift up the Son of Man, you will know that 'I Am Who I Am'; then you will know that I do nothing on my own authority, but I say only what the Father has instructed me to say.

29 And he who sent me is with me; he has not left me alone, because I always do what pleases him."

- John 8:27-29 (TEV)

It is no wonder that our Lord Jesus Christ had power and authority over all things. He would want us Christians to be empowered like Him.

49 And I myself will send upon you what my Father has promised. But you must wait in the city until the power from above comes down upon you."

- Luke 24:49 (TEV)

8 But when the Holy Spirit comes upon you, you will be filled with power, and you will be witnesses for me

in Jerusalem, in all of Judea and Samaria, and to the ends of the earth."
- Acts 1:8 (TEV)

And soon after He rose from the dead, He appeared to His disciples and said to them:

21 Jesus said to them again, "Peace be with you. As the Father sent me, so I send you."

22 Then he breathed on them and said, "Receive the Holy Spirit.
John 20:21-22 (TEV)

Facing Persecution

There is a need for endurance. Let's take two examples of empowerment.

1. Our Lord Jesus Christ

"Looking unto Jesus, the author, and finisher of our faith, who for the joy that was set before Him endured

the cross, despising the shame, and has sat down at the right hand of the throne of God."
- *Hebrews 12:2 (KJV)*

2. The Apostle Paul

'But thou hast fully known my doctrine, manner of life, purpose, faith, longsuffering, charity, patience, persecutions, afflictions, which came unto me at Antioch, at Iconium, at Lystra; what persecutions I endured: but out of them all the Lord delivered me.'
- *2 Timothy 3:10-11 (KJV)*

You and I must pray for the grace to endure whatever persecution we face while eagerly waiting for heaven to intervene. On empowerment proper, we must go to the Prophet Micah for inspiration in Micah 3:8:

'But truly I am full of power by the Spirit of the Lord, and of justice and might, to declare to Jacob his transgression And to Israel his sin.'

We must believe and receive the resurrection power of Jesus and apply it to our world as we exercise the spiritual authority given to us by our Lord Jesus Christ.

19 and how very great is his power at work in us who believe. This power working in us is the same as the mighty strength

20 which he used when he raised Christ from death and seated him at his right side in the heavenly world.

21 Christ rules there above all heavenly rulers, authorities, powers, and lords; he has a title superior to all titles of authority in this world and in the next.

22 God put all things under Christ's feet and gave him to the church as supreme Lord over all things.

23 The church is Christ's body, the completion of him who himself completes all things everywhere.

- Ephesians 1:19-23 (TEV)

There is a way to possess what we have received from the spiritual realm. This is fundamental. The Bible says, "*If you confess that Jesus is Lord and believe that God raised Him from the dead, you will be saved." (Romans 10:9)*

For it is by our faith that we are put right with God, not by our works. What you believe in your heart puts you right with God. God sees the heart. When a man believes in Jesus Christ as his Lord and Saviour, his name moves from God's Book of Judgment to God's Book of Life.

To possess the benefits of his faith in Christ, he must confess that Jesus Christ is his Lord and Saviour. *Confession leads to possession*. And the more you confess, the more you possess. When Micah says, *"I am full of power by the Spirit of God and of courage and of might"*, he is confessing what he believes in his heart, which heaven has noticed. As he speaks about it and declares it to be so, there is a release of power from heaven to actualize it on earth.

So believe first that God has empowered you with resurrection power since our Lord Jesus Christ rose from the grave. And to possess that power, confess that you have it in you, and heaven will endorse it. The power becomes available when we confess that we have it.

The lesson is in Mark 11:24 (KJV):

24Therefore I say unto you, What things soever ye desire, when ye pray, believe that ye receive them, and ye shall have them.

That's the way the spiritual empowerment system works. The Scripture says, believe when you pray because there's a faithful God who answers prayer. There's a God of love who desires that His purposes be established in and through our lives. He wants us to surmount the opposition and go through the world, victorious through the power released and made available to us after Christ rose from the grave. When we pray, we believe we receive God's power and the courage and boldness to act, and we will have what we believe.

There is a practical lesson in this. Suppose a man comes to work in an office and notices that something evil is going on there: He should first go to God in prayer to say, "*O Lord, what do You want me to do? How do You want me to proceed?* When he gets his marching orders, he returns to God again to ask for courage and boldness: *Spirit of the living God, the giver of boldness, I ask for and receive boldness from You now.*" And then, he opens his mouth and begins to carry out the divine plan for change, and everybody says, "*Wow! Where did he find such courage?*" He found it in the quickening of the Holy Spirit, and that's the way we function. That's the way to face opposition.

To checkmate opposition and control persecution, he can also say a pre-emptive prayer: *"Lord, I take authority over every opposing spirit here. I bind them with fetters of iron, and I confine them."* Let us listen to our Lord Jesus Christ on this:

"No one can break into a strong man's house and take away his belongings unless he first ties up the strong man; then he can plunder his house.
- Mark 3:27 (TEV)

We learn to tie up the strong man of persecution and opposition before we engage so that we can do what we should do unhindered like our Lord Jesus Christ:

Now about the middle of the feast Jesus went up into the temple and taught. And the Jews marveled, saying, "How does this Man know letters, having never studied?"
- John 7:14-15 (NKJV)

Now some of them from Jerusalem said, "Is this not He whom they seek to kill? But look! He speaks boldly, and they say nothing to Him. Do the rulers know indeed that this is truly the Christ?

- John 7:25-26 (NKJV)

Our Lord Jesus delayed His appearance at the feast in Jerusalem until heaven deployed His divine protection. You and I should do the same. Let us learn to walk like our Lord Jesus Christ: that way, we never become sitting ducks for the enemy to pluck us one after the other. We are empowered to resist all the forces of persecution and cause them to be subject to Christ. This authority will protect us from unnecessary persecution by men and devils. A man can walk into a place and say, *"I command every thought and opinion here to be subject to Christ, in the name of Jesus."* And then, he looks up to heaven because he has expectations that the Spirit of God will come and take over the place. The more we practice this in our lives, the more we will have testimonies of how God prevailed. This is exactly what Apostle Paul was saying, *"I endured affliction for some time, but God came and delivered me from all of them."*

CONFESSION

Let us do this like Prophet Micah:

I am filled with resurrection power now to dethrone all principalities, all powers, all the rulers of darkness in this world, and all spiritual wickedness in high places. I take authority over all hindrances to the purposes of God in my life today. I shall walk daily by the power of the Spirit of God to fulfill God's purposes through my life, in Jesus name, I pray, Amen.

My God is able to do exceedingly, abundantly above all, that I can ever ask or think according to the power that He has deposited in me to cause His will and purposes to be established in me and through me in Jesus matchless name, Amen.

I urge you to start confessing this today and every day, and you will be amazed at how God is giving you victory on the road of life. You will be bold in the face of any opposition. Keep this confession separate from your other prayer times because of Matthew 6:7-8 that admonishes, *"When you pray do not use a lot of meaningless words as the pagans do. You will think that their gods will hear them because their prayers are long. Do not be like them for your Father already knows what you need before you ask Him."*

We come to our prayer time to receive power because we cannot face the opposition in our strength or will power. As we seek empowerment, God's wisdom is distilled to us to confound the enemy. There is no magic to this, brothers and sisters; by the grace that comes through faith, we are made overcomers through our Lord Jesus Christ.

PRAYER

Father, here I am, an empty vessel. O God, fill me with Yourself. Fill me with the knowledge of Christ, fill me with Your Holy Spirit and give me Your inner strength, the courage, and wisdom to come against all opposition to establish the Kingdom of God and its righteousness on this earth, in Jesus' precious name I pray. Amen.

ABOUT THE AUTHOR

Dr. Okey Onuzo is a Consultant Nephrologist and the pioneer physician of the first private dialysis center in Nigeria to treat patients with kidney failure and related conditions. Life Support Medical Centre opened its doors to patients officially on October 4, 1986. He was trained both in Nigeria and the USA.

Dr. Onuzo received the Lord Jesus Christ as his personal Lord and Saviour on June 28, 1970, at a guest invitational service. On the night of June 28, he had a vivid dream where a voice asked him to wake up and read John 6:20. That Scripture reads, "*It is I, be not afraid.*" That was his first encounter with the Lord Jesus Christ. It changed his life entirely and set him on a course to know the One who has called him.

In 1973, at an anointing service at the University of Ibadan in Nigeria, he received an apostolic calling with emphasis on the teaching and the prophetic ministries. He has watched over the years as the Holy Spirit has exposed and expanded these callings to touch several lives in different parts of the world.

Dr. Onuzo has authored several books that try to survey various dimensions of the Spirit-led life. He is generally acknowledged as a conference and seminar speaker, and minister of God's word. Formerly, the Associate Pastor of the National Headquarter Church of the Foursquare Gospel Church in Nigeria; pioneer chapter President of the Full Gospel Business Men's Fellowship International (FGBMFI), Ikeja in 1986 from which he rose to become a National

Director of the Fellowship in Nigeria, before stepping aside in the year 2000.

Currently, he serves as the President, Life Link Worldwide Ministries. He runs the Kingdom Life Seminars to raise a community of believers, disciples who desire to follow in the footprints of our Lord Jesus Christ.

He is married to Mariam, a medical doctor, and they have four children: Dilichi, Chinaza, Dinachi, and Chibundu.

BOOKS BY OKEY ONUZO

1. The Convert and the Counsellor

2. Pathway to Conversational Prayers

3. You May Kiss the Bride: Choice, Engagement, Courtship, Marriage, Divorce, Remarriage, Polygamy-- and the Christian

4. Dimensions of Faith

5. Minspi

6. God's Will, The Way to Power

7. You May Kiss the Bride: Choice and Marriage

8. Spiritual Intelligence

9. The Beatitudes: The Spiritual Overhauling Kit

Made in the USA
Columbia, SC
23 October 2021